JULIO HERRERA Y REISSIG
AND THE SYMBOLISTS

Julio Herrera y Reissig and the Symbolists

BY BERNARD GICOVATE

UNIVERSITY OF CALIFORNIA PRESS
BERKELEY AND LOS ANGELES   1957

University of California Press
Berkeley and Los Angeles

Cambridge University Press
London, England

Copyright, 1957, by
The Regents of the University of California

PREFACE

A technical study of poetry seems to require an excuse in these days. But there is seldom any excuse to offer. For this monograph I am tempted to invoke the propitiating consideration that the poetry of Julio Herrera y Reissig has been the subject of controversy. If I add that Herrera y Reissig is little known outside Spanish America, the excuse looks only a little less trifling. There is always too long a road to traverse: the historical setting, the poet's intellectual milieu, his apprenticeship, and his later achievements must all be dealt with. The originality of a poem, however, cannot be apprehended except in its own terms.

The work of Herrera y Reissig is of interest because of its very eccentricity. Lying somewhat tangential to the poet's own culture and closely related to another, it offers an opportunity for the study of the strange quickening produced in an alert mind when it comes in contact with a foreign culture. For this reason, even though it does not always achieve a mature blending of its elements—the poet died at the age of thirty-five—Herrera's poetry is rewarding.

The poet's personality and life were as paradoxical as his works. Although he lived intensely, Herrera y Reissig hardly has a biography, biographers notwithstanding. He was born and died in Montevideo, a city he seldom left and then only for short vacations in the Uruguayan countryside. His single adventure in travel was pitifully dull: he spent a few months in

Buenos Aires as a clerk. Only in imagination and through his readings did he taste the fanciful pleasures of European Decadence. He was not, of course, a Decadent by medical advice; yet the addiction to morphine that shocked his countrymen was the result of a physiological need arising from a malformation of the heart. Even Herrera's Bohemianism was cultivated in the security of his father's middle-class home and, after his father died, in the home of his wife's parents. He presided over a little *cénacle* for which he could find no larger meeting place than a garret in his father's home. But the poet took revenge on fate and bequeathed to Uruguayan literary history the most pompous name for a salon. To his "Torre de los Panoramas" came a few young men to be encouraged in their search for novelties and refinements. No literary prizes or diplomatic posts were offered to their mentor. In isolation, Herrera's mind grew crotchety, his poetry esoteric, at times unintelligible. And yet, less than five decades after his death, Herrera y Reissig is considered the first modern poet of Uruguay.

In the course of my research on the works of Herrera y Reissig and the immediate task of writing, countless persons, many unknowingly, have lent assistance. It is a pleasure to acknowledge in particular the aid of the late Professor Amado Alonso and of Professor Renato Poggioli of Harvard University, of Professor Chandler B. Beall of the University of Oregon, and of Professor Arturo Torres-Ríoseco of the University of California.

CONTENTS

I *Modernismo* and Its Relation to French Poetry   1

II Influences in the Works of Herrera y Reissig   18

III From Image to Myth: The Impasse of Symbolism   39

IV The Early Poems of Herrera y Reissig   54

V A Private Diction   62

VI Experiments in Structure   82

    Notes   93

    Bibliography   97

    Index   105

CHAPTER I

MODERNISMO AND ITS RELATION

TO FRENCH POETRY

Julio Herrera y Reissig made his poetic contribution at the end of a distinct period in Spanish American letters. His work was not only his creation but also the product of a milieu conditioned by historical processes. The cultural atmosphere of the times in which Herrera lived and the important antecedents of his experiments help to explain the complexity of his poetic world and lay the groundwork for an evaluation of his achievement.

During the colonial centuries, foreign influences came to Spanish America mainly through Spanish channels, but in the last two hundred years inspiration has been derived primarily from French sources. In the chaotic early decades of the nineteenth century, when the desire for political independence began to stir, Romantic influences were felt in Spanish America before they were accepted on the Spanish Peninsula. In the second half of the century, when governments in Spanish America became more stable, cultural development was possible, and the conscientious artist succeeded the writer of patriotic verse and of political pamphlets. The New World reached maturity in the search for intellectual independence when, at the end of the nineteenth century, its writers carried *fin de siècle* ideas and innovations to Spain.

The last two decades of the nineteenth century and the first of the twentieth—a literary period known as *modernismo*—were years of tireless creation. In poetry, especially, there was a development of unprecedented variety and force that culminated in the works of Rubén Darío. Poets were led by his example to study recent French poetry; they learned from his works to adapt foreign innovations to the Spanish language. The poetry of Julio Herrera y Reissig, written in the first decade of the twentieth century, is characteristic of the general assimilation of *Parnasse*, Decadence, and Symbolism. Because of the poet's personal isolation and early death, his works illustrate a well-defined period of the infiltration of French Symbolism in the literary history of Spanish America.

Modernismo before Rubén Darío

To find new means of poetic expression was only one of the aspirations of Spanish American writers in the years from 1880 to 1905. They also attempted to educate the reading public, and endeavored to bring their countries into the contemporary patterns of European culture. They faced the twofold task of creation and of cultural diffusion. The latter was effected through articles in established periodicals dealing with recent foreign trends and books, and the publication of numerous ephemeral magazines devoted to the study and translation of late nineteenth-century French literature.

In Spanish America, Romantic writing lingered long after the battle of Neoclassics and Romantics had been won by the younger generations. Twelve years after *Hernani*, this battle took the form of a literary polemic in the periodicals of Santiago de Chile between the followers of Andrés Bello and those of

Domingo Faustino Sarmiento. The latter was a disciple of Esteban Echeverría, who had introduced Romanticism into the River Plate region upon his return from France in 1830. As late as 1867, when French Realism was already being imported into Chile as a literary method by Alberto Blest Gana, there appeared the most famous Romantic novel of Spanish America, *María*, by the Colombian Jorge Isaacs.

A peculiar Spanish offshoot of Romanticism, *costumbrismo*, was also transplanted and became very popular in Spanish America. Together with *costumbrista* sketches, works of larger scope in vernacular dialect were written. Gauchesque literature—an attempt to create a national literature in the vernacular of the River Plate region—may be viewed as a consequence of Romanticism. The masterpiece of this type in the nineteenth century is the narrative poem *Martín Fierro* (1872–1879) by José Hernández, which derives its powerful simplicity from the tradition of Spanish popular poetry. In contrast, the poetry in standard Spanish was imitative and grandiloquent, usually in the manner of Victor Hugo, Ramón de Campoamor, and Núñez de Arce, as, for instance, the patriotic odes of the Argentine Olegario Víctor Andrade.

The younger generation directed their iconoclastic zeal against the imitative poetry and excessive localism of their elders. Although they had begun writing under the direction of Zorrilla, Campoamor, and Núñez de Arce, the *modernistas*, in their revolutionary impatience, rejected most of the immediate past, except for the works of Gustavo Adolfo Bécquer, whose aesthetics[1] and poetry are, in the Spanish world, an intimation of Symbolism.

The renewal of poetic diction was heralded by a generation of precursors working in the 'eighties and early 'nineties. José Martí (1853–1895), whose *Ismaelillo* (1882) is considered the first collection of poetry of the *modernista* movement, was the only one better acquainted with English and American than with French literature. Through Martí's essays on Emerson, Bronson Alcott, Walt Whitman, and his own works written under their influence, the movement was enriched with Transcendentalist ideas. Yet Martí's poetry owes most of its simple intensity to his familiarity with the masters of the Golden Age—Santa Teresa was his favorite author—and to the stream of popular Spanish poetry kept alive in the New World.

Other important Spanish American precursors of *modernismo* were Julián del Casal, Manuel Gutiérrez Nájera, and José Asunción Silva. Their writings circled the poles of exotic escape and Bohemian revolt, voicing discontent and pessimism. Although only Silva traveled in France, all three were familiar with French literature and introduced into their respective countries the innovations of the late Romantics and the Parnassians. French influence in their work was, however, superficial; it had not been incorporated in a unified aesthetic conception. Scattered among their lines are traces of the exquisite workmanship of Gautier, the Satanism of Baudelaire, the exoticism of Leconte de Lisle or even Loti, the humanitarianism of Coppée, the melancholy of Gustavo Adolfo Bécquer, and the pessimism of Leopardi and Schopenhauer.

The Cuban Julián del Casal (1863–1893) wrote in the manner of Heredia and Leconte de Lisle in his most successful poems. Casal reflects also the contemporary interest in late nineteenth-century French painters: the mythological subjects of Gustave Moreau's Decadent paintings are described precisely and colorfully in the sonnet series *Mi museo ideal*. In his worship of craftsmanship and objectivity, Casal followed the tenets of the Parnassians.

The poetry of Casal in relation to that of Baudelaire is a clear example of failure to assimilate an aesthetic conception, in spite of the poet's admiration for his model. Casal alludes to Baudelaire's works in his own writings:

> ... las frías
> hermosuras de estériles senos
> que, cual flores del mal, han caído
> de la vida al oscuro sendero.[2]

Casal's "La canción de la morfina" was inspired by Baudelaire's concern with *les paradis artificiels:*

> Amantes de la quimera,
> yo calmaré vuestro mal:
> soy la dicha artificial,
> que es la dicha verdadera.[2]

In "Nostalgias" he follows Baudelaire in the theme of escape "anywhere out of this world." He shares with his French master a preference for cities over the country. But never does his poem create the evocative reality that emerges from Baudelaire's sensuous lines.

Casal contributed to the task of cultural diffusion by publishing translations of some of the prose poems of Baudelaire and Catulle Mendès and by writing on figures of the *fin de siècle*. His translations, elegantly done but not always exact, and his rapid impressions of Guy de Maupassant and J. K. Huysmans, among others, appeared in *La Habana Elegante* in 1886 and 1887 and were, like his imitations of Gautier, Coppée, and Heredia, important steps in the education of the reading public. In "Kakemono" he echoed the Japanese exoticism of Judith Gautier and Loti.

Manuel Gutiérrez Nájera (1859–1896) is credited with the introduction of *fin de siècle* trends in Mexico. In the magazine he edited, *Revista Azul* (1894–1896), appeared translations of Baudelaire, Catulle Mendès, Coppée, Loti, Heredia, Verlaine, and others. The adjective "azul" had already become a favorite with *modernistas* after the success of Darío's *Azul . . .* (1888), but Nájera had already published some poems entitled "Del Libro Azul" (1880).

The poetry of Nájera was written under the influence of Romantics and Parnassians, mainly Alfred de Musset and Théophile Gautier, whose "Symphonie en blanc majeur" was the model for Nájera's "De blanco." His facile verse, playful wit, and genius for the sentimental story made his pen name, "El Duque Job," popular in Mexico. Imitations, reminiscences, and even fragmentary translations are common in his poetry. He did not hesitate to include in his poem "Para un menú" a paraphrase of the last lines of Louis Bouilhet's "Vers à une femme."³ He imitated Coppée, and was an admirer of Mendès. Nájera was so thoroughly imbued with French letters that he considered himself an expatriate in Mexico. His example and his direct advocacy of *cruzamiento*⁴ in literature directed Mexican youth toward the avid reading and imitation of foreign writers.

José Asunción Silva (1865-1896), who had in his adolescent writings followed Hugo, Byron, Musset, and Bécquer, and who initiated the *modernista* movement in his native Colombia, is the most complex and original personality of his generation. Silva had read Verlaine, Mallarmé, and D'Annunzio, and in his conversations and recitations introduced his Bogotá friends to their works as well as to the writings of Dante Gabriel Rossetti, Flaubert, Maupassant, Baudelaire, Rimbaud, and Villiers de l'Isle-Adam, whose books he had brought from Europe. In his poetry the main influences are Heine, Poe,⁵ Baudelaire, Bécquer, Bartrina, and Campoamor. His spleen—which ended in suicide—was nurtured in the pessimistic readings he mentions:

> Luego, desencantado de la vida,
> filósofo sutil,
> a Leopardi leyó, y a Schopenhauer
> y en un rato de spleen,
> se curó para siempre con las cápsulas
> de plomo de un fusil.⁶

Of the precursors, Silva was the most conscientious artist and the one best acquainted with European literature, especially with the English Pre-Raphaelites and the French Decadents. In his loosely autobiographical novel *De sobremesa* he defends the Decadents in his discussion of Max Nordau's *Degeneration*. His best poems were written in the late 'eighties and in the 'nineties, after Darío had become the acknowledged master of *modernismo*, a fact which decreases some of their importance in the development of Spanish American literature. Toward the end of his life he became concerned with musicality—in a vague, Verlainean sense—and with sound, color, and perfume effects and relationships:

> Junté sílabas dulces, como el sabor
>   de un beso,
> bordé las frases de oro, les di
>   música extraña,
> . . . .
> les di olor de heliotropos y color
>   de amatista . . .⁶

These lines probably refer to his famous "Nocturno," one of the most successful *modernista* poems, written in a novel metrical pattern, based on a four-syllable foot repeated freely from two to six times, with the occasional interpolation of a two-syllable foot, and with subtle assonance.

Some poets of the same generation are worthy of mention for their attempts to introduce foreign innovations. Manuel González Prada (1844-1918), of Peru, tried to revitalize old metrical forms such as the triolet and rondel. The Mexican Parnassians, Manuel José Othón (1858-1906) and Salvador Díaz Mirón (1853-1928), and Leopoldo Díaz (1862-1947), a Parnassian writer of the Argentine, carried this kind of poetry into the twentieth century. In Spain the same type of change was brought about by Manuel Reina (1856-1905), Ricardo Gil (1855-1908), and Salvador Rueda (1857-1933). On the whole, the poets of the Spanish Peninsula were less interested in French literature than were the Spanish Americans, and more familiar with the great medieval and Golden Age masters.

From *Azul* . . . to *Cantos de vida y esperanza*

With the exception of José Asunción Silva, in a few of his poems, and José Martí, who wrote little poetry, the precursors, after the initial enthusiasm subsided, have become writers of mainly historical and local interest. Nevertheless, their effort made possible the new movement and the subsequent development of poetry in the twentieth century. It remained for Rubén Darío (1867-1916) to bring together all the aspirations of his times and produce the great poetry they had prepared. In his works, for the first time in the history of the Spanish language, a new poetic message is carried to the mother country by a Spanish American who is universally conceded to be the master of a movement. Some aspects of Darío's works may substantiate the belief in an extreme dependence on his extensive French readings. He had great admiration for the masters of the Golden Age, however, and believed that he was the continuator of "Cervantes y Calderones"; he expressed, also, the emotion and the voice of his America.

The successive stages of Rubén Darío's response to European literature determined the course of the *modernista* movement. The successful assimilation of the French *Parnasse* was achieved in 1888 in his first important book, *Azul* . . . , previously published in fragmentary form in the periodicals *La Epoca*, *Revista de Artes y Letras*, and *La Libertad Electoral* of Santiago de Chile between December 7, 1886, and July 23, 1888. Thereafter the writers of *la mêlée symboliste* were studied and imitated in Spanish America. *Los raros* (1896), a collection of articles written for *La Nación*, was Darío's contribution to the widening of literary horizons in Spanish America. His *Prosas profanas* (1896) were tinged with Decadence; but after 1898, partly as a result of the Spanish-American War, most writers of the Spanish world were concerned with immediate social, historical, and political problems.

In *Historia de mis libros,*[1] Darío explained that the title *Azul* . . . did not originate in Hugo's phrase "l'art c'est l'azur," which he did not know when he wrote this book, but was inspired by a stanza in *Les Châtiments:*
> Adieu, patrie!
> L'onde est en furie.
> Adieu, patrie,
> Azur!

There may also have been, although Darío does not mention it, a reminiscence of Mallarmé's poem "L'Azur," which he had read in *Le Parnasse Contemporain* (1866). At that time the poetry of Mallarmé was still in accord with the aesthetic attitude of the *Parnasse*—the school Darío followed; the Symbolists were not yet known in Spanish America.[2] Among the French authors to whom Darío acknowledges his indebtedness, the most important are Victor Hugo, Catulle Mendès, Théophile Gautier, Leconte de Lisle, Armand Silvestre, Flaubert, Daudet, and Zola; the influence of Zola is apparent only in the naturalistic tale "El fardo."

The exquisite exoticism and erotic refinement of "La ninfa" and "El pájaro azul," laid in an imaginary Paris of elegance and of Bohemianism, characterize the collection. In "La muerte de la emperatriz de la China," added in the edition of 1900, the elements of Oriental exoticism were derived from Judith Gautier and Pierre Loti. *Azul* . . . includes erotic tales of autobiographical inspiration, "Palomas blancas y garzas morenas," and many pictorial sketches. In the edition of 1900, several "Medallones" were added; these sonnets in honor of other poets indicate the objects of the young Darío's admiration: "Leconte de Lisle," "Catulle Mendès," "Walt Whitman," "J. J. Palma" (a contemporary Cuban poet), and "Salvador Díaz Mirón." The contradictory homage to the "good, grey poet," in a book of aristocratic refinement, may be considered a result of immaturity. Later, in the preface to *Prosas profanas*, Darío rejected the democratic inspiration of Walt Whitman.

On the basis of several Alexandrine sonnets in *Azul...*, Darío later maintained that he had introduced this pattern into Spanish; there had been one antecedent, however, in the seventeenth-century sonnet "Como el triste piloto que por el mar incierto," by Pedro de Espinosa. Darío's attempt was, nevertheless, independent of Espinosa's poem, published in a modern edition in 1909.⁹ This metrical pattern became popular after *Azul...*, and, continuing a trend that had begun with the Romantics, the Alexandrine in other patterns was revitalized after having been virtually forgotten since the Middle Ages, when, in the *tetrástrofo monorrimo*, it had been the rhythm commonly used by poets of the *mester de clerecía*.

Although it contained mostly prose tales and sketches and only six poems in the first edition, *Azul...* revolutionized the poetry of its day. The author became famous in the Spanish world after the publication of Juan Valera's critical comments in *El Imparcial* of October 22, 1888. Valera defined the novelty in a fortunate phrase, "galicismo mental," emphasizing the fact that Darío seemed to think naturally in French, but mistakenly asserting that his language was in no way Gallicized.¹⁰ Darío later summarized the qualities of his youthful Gallicism:

El *Azul...* es un libro parnasiano, y por lo tanto, francés. En él aparecen por primera vez en nuestra lengua, el "cuento" parisiense, la adjetivación francesa, el giro galo injertado en el párrafo castellano: la chuchería de Goncourt, la *câlinerie* erótica de Mendès, el encogimiento verbal de Heredia, y hasta un poquito de Coppée.¹¹

Among the sketches in the series "Cuadros," "Un retrato de Watteau" reveals the fascination of aristocratic eighteenth-century France for the Spanish American poet, who must have acquired his Decadent artistic tastes from the brothers Goncourt. In "La canción del oro," modeled after Baudelaire's

"Litanies de Satan," and "El rey burgués," the denunciation of bourgeois society, a recurring theme in *Azul* . . . , is explicit. Antibourgeois feelings, refined eroticism, interest in the eighteenth century, ivory-tower disdain of the average, are traits Darío shared with some of the Decadents whom he discussed later in *Los raros*.[12] The motley array of personalities this book presented in rapid impressionistic sketches have not all resisted the passage of half a century and were not equally important in the development of Darío's poetry, which was being published in periodicals at the same time. These poems, collected later in *Prosas profanas* (1896), spread the influence of the French Decadents in the Spanish world. Verlaine became the model of the Spanish American poet, who mentions him along with Moréas and Dante Gabriel Rossetti in *Historia de mis libros*.

In *Prosas profanas*, Darío moved away from an almost exclusive interest in the visual arts in order to follow the dictates of Verlaine's "Art poétique." Verlaine had already declared[13] his opposition to the Symbolist group; and the distinction between the esoteric search for the "sens plus pur," indefatigably pursued by Mallarmé, and the worship of "la musique avant toute chose" of Verlaine's followers was clear.

Darío's affinities with Verlaine prevented him from adhering to Mallarmé's group: "Si soy verleniano no puedo ser moreista, o mallarmista, pues son maneras distintas,"[14] he declared. He knew, however, the values to be found in Mallarmé's poetry, and wrote a penetrating discussion of his works for *El Mercurio de América* in 1898. It seems that Darío had only recently made a more complete study of Mallarmé. *Los raros* had included only a few passing references to him, and the quotation of one line of the early poem "Brise marine," published in *Le Parnasse Contemporain* of May 12, 1866: "La chair est triste, hélas! et j'ai lu tous les livres." The title *Prosas profanas*, in which the word "prosa" is used in its medieval meaning (as exemplified by Berceo's line,

"Quiero fer una prosa en román paladino"), apparently has no connection with Mallarmé's "proses." Knowledge of the works of Mallarmé was at this time only fragmentary in the Spanish world, and his influence was secondary to that of the Decadents, who were the directing force in *modernista* poetry. *Un Coup de dés* was not translated until 1919,[14] when Mallarmé was hailed as master of the avant-garde poets. The extreme esotericism of Mallarmé's late works and the historical events of the end of the century probably accounted for the delay in the assimilation of his poetic discoveries.

The use of symbols in the poetry of Rubén Darío is rather in the manner of traditional allegory than in accord with Symbolist aesthetics. The allegorical procedure is clear in the interpretation of the symbolic elements which the poet offers in the poem "El reino interior," influenced by Rossetti: "Y esas bellas princesas son las siete virtudes."

The most important innovation of *Prosas profanas* was the rich variety of meters, some of them new to the Spanish language, as in the combination of Alexandrines and nine-syllable lines in the "Responso a Verlaine." Old meters acquired new musicality: the nine-syllable line was revived, the ten- and twelve-syllable lines were made more flexible. The hendecasyllable readmitted lost varieties, such as the *endecasílabo de gaita gallega* and the *mínimo*, with accents on the seventh and the fourth syllables, respectively. Irregular combinations, and even approximations to free verse, are among the innovations introduced by Rubén Darío, some of them inspired by the metrical patterns of French poetry.

In 1898, two years after the publication of *Prosas profanas*, Rubén Darío visited Spain for the second time. During his earlier stay, in 1892, the poet had found little interest in the new poetry, but this time a group of young writers in Madrid were engaged in what was later recognized as a renaissance of Spanish intellectual life. The poets of this group, which came to be known as the "Generation of '98," welcomed the influence from the New World. Their renewal of Spanish poetry was in its turn to be carried across the Atlantic to the younger writers of Spanish America.

Among the Spanish poets Francisco Villaespesa, Manuel and Antonio Machado, Juan Ramón Jiménez, Ramón María del Valle Inclán, and others, a phase of the movement that had been, in Spanish America, secondary to the importation of French culture emerged anew: the renewal of poetry through the use of themes and forms of the popular and medieval literature of Spain. The interest in medieval studies—a trend that dates from the late eighteenth century—was part of the spirit of the times. Gonzalo de Berceo, Juan Ruiz, Santillana, and Gil Vicente were studied and reinterpreted. The revival of Góngora started another literary current early in the century, culminating in the late 'twenties in the work of such scholars as Millé y Giménez, Miguel Artigas, Dámaso Alonso, and the Mexican Alfonso Reyes.

Modernismo had long been accepted in Spanish America, but in Spain the traditionalists, and even some members of the Generation of '98, voiced their hostility to the movement. The leadership of Unamuno, who vehemently opposed *modernismo*, both conflicted with and supplemented the influence of Rubén Darío on the new poetry in Spain.[16] Spanish American expressions of *modernismo* are the result of cosmopolitan and aesthetic interests, in opposition to the graver ideological and national concerns of Spanish writers.

By the nature of its revolutionary force, the *modernista* movement was destined to undergo constant change. The somber atmosphere of Madrid influenced Rubén Darío, who turned to the immediate problems of "his country." For him this meant the whole Spanish world, and he sang, in some of the *Cantos de vida y esperanza* (1905), of his "ínclitas razas ubérrimas." This book marks the end of *modernismo* as a period of assimilation of foreign literatures. Thereafter Rubén Darío moved into new fields. The disintegration of the movement produced varied results: an exaggerated *americanismo*—a trend sometimes called *mundonovismo*—in the works of José Santos Chocano and lesser poets; a series of reactions (1905–1914) that attempted to return to older aesthetic forms; and an attempt at renewal and further development that leads into the avant-garde poetry of the postwar period. Darío himself continued to write, and pointed the way for many of his successors with "Canto a la Argentina" (1910), a masterpiece of *mundonovismo*. In *El canto errante* (1907) and *Poema del otoño y otros poemas* (1910), his poetry is enriched with a new irony, a deeper disillusionment, and the use of deliberate prosaisms.

The movement synthesized by Rubén Darío carried its message into all the capitals of the Spanish world and revolutionized the writing of every Spanish-speaking country. A study of literary evolution in Spanish countries in this period must include the relation of their writers to the poetry of Rubén Darío and the foreign influences he introduced. Of Darío's numerous disciples in the River Plate region, where he lived and wrote at intervals, the Uruguayan Julio Herrera y Reissig was one of the forceful personalities who, "por caminos ajenos y por caminos propios,"[17] made further innovations.

Modernismo in Uruguay

The cultural history of the Republic of Uruguay differs slightly from the general pattern of Spanish America. By 1888 the cultural lag which the *modernistas* were trying to overcome was much more pronounced in that country. Uruguayan writers were still imitating the European Romantics while the precursors of *modernismo* were already engaged in studying the Parnassians and the Decadents, and novelists had been observing and recording in the manner of the Realists for twenty years. *Modernista* writing was at first confined to the countries north of the Equator, while Realism had its start in Chile. The River Plate region came later into the *modernista* movement and, when it did, literary development centered in Buenos Aires.

Historically, the delay in the cultural development of Uruguay may be explained by its late settlement and colonization, and, during the nineteenth century, its proximity to and dependence on Buenos Aires, which influenced Uruguayan tastes and attracted young men of talent from Uruguay, who often became part of the literary life of Argentina.

It is peculiar to Uruguay that Realism and Naturalism in fiction, Positivism in education and philosophical thinking, and *modernismo* in poetry and the essay were all introduced at the same time, in spite of their conflicting attitudes. The antipositivist Decadent and the deterministic Naturalist felt united against the academic success of the Romanticists. *Tabaré*, by Juan Zorrilla de San Martín, was published in 1888, and the outmoded credo typified by this Indianist narrative aroused the opposition of the young. In this poem, a verse rendition of the idyllic Indian novel that had been popular in Spanish America for several decades, the author tried to imitate the melancholy tone of Bécquer's poetry. The popular success of *Tabaré* has never been equaled in Uruguay, although twentieth-century criticism has not been favorable.

The first *modernistas* appeared in Uruguay in March, 1895, with the publication of the *Revista Nacional de Literatura y Ciencias Sociales*, edited by José Enrique Rodó, Víctor Pérez Petit, and Daniel and Carlos Martínez Vigil. Uruguay now entered fully into the cultural life of Spanish America, even, at times, directing it through the powerful personality of the ethical thinker and literary critic José Enrique Rodó. The *modernistas* of Uruguay were influenced from the start by the Decadents and by Rubén Darío's *Prosas profanas*. Some, however, wrote Parnassian poetry. Belatedly, in 1907, when Herrera y Reissig was already writing Symbolist poems, Víctor Pérez Petit wrote his Parnassian *Joyeles bárbaros*.

The work of cultural diffusion undertaken by the *Revista Nacional* was nonacademic in nature, since Uruguay did not then have a school of the humanities comparable to those of the other Spanish American countries. The first Uruguayan *modernistas* presented in their reviews the personalities of Ibsen, Tolstoy, Hauptmann, Nietzsche, D'Annunzio, Verlaine, Mallarmé, Eugenio de Castro, and the original work of Rubén Darío and his disciples, principally Ricardo Jaimes Freyre and the Argentine poet Leopoldo Lugones, who was then engaged in imitations of several French poets.

In spite of its nonacademic character, the movement started with reflective and critical writing. The leader of the group, José Enrique Rodó, was, under the influence of Taine, one of the first exponents of positivist criticism in Spanish America. His writings on the nineteenth-century development of Spanish American literature are still masterpieces of historical reconstruction. His first contribution to the criticism of *modernismo* was his famous essay of 1899 on Rubén Darío, in which he declared that Darío was not the poet of America. The assertion was perhaps valid at that time, and may have influenced Darío to turn to poetry expressing the emotions of his homeland. Rodó's *Ariel*, of 1900, reminiscent of Renan's *Caliban*, influenced the direction of Spanish American thinking in the early twentieth century. This intellectual breviary called Spanish American youth to a balanced life of the mind, in opposition to the exclusively materialistic interests which Rodó believed democracies, especially the United States, entertained. In its aristocratic tendency, its Gallicized Hellenism, the book follows *modernista* trends. Yet its political significance places it in the third phase of the movement.

In November, 1897, when the *Revista Nacional* ceased publication, a small group of enthusiastic Bohemians founded the Centro Internacional de Estudios Sociales, a club that advocated "el individuo libre en la comunidad libre."[8] Their freedom was to be unlimited; they believed in political anarchism and free love and, naturally, were not easily accepted by the bourgeois of quiet Montevideo. Of this group only Florencio Sánchez, who later became a playwright in the Argentine, eventually gave successful artistic expression to his ideas of social reform.

These Bohemian groups constituted, for a few years, the most important literary life of Uruguay. Their meeting places, besides the Centro, were two literary clubs, the Consistorio del Gay Saber and La Torre de los Panoramas. In the Consistorio, Horacio Quiroga, who was later to win acclaim for his tales of the Argentine jungles, was followed by a group of young rebels, while the solitary figure of Julio Herrera y Reissig entertained a few admirers in La Torre de los Panoramas.

Out of the Consistorio came the first book of Decadent poetry published in Uruguay, Horacio Quiroga's *Los arrecifes de coral* (1901), which the critics received with unanimous disapproval. It had been preceded by the Decadent prose of Uruguay's colorful dandy, Roberto de las Carreras. In 1899, under the influence of Pierre Louÿs, D'Annunzio, and the Colombian Vargas Vila, De las Carreras wrote *Sueño de Oriente*, a pamphlet that ridiculed Montevidean society and expounded unwelcome theories of free love. When this book reached the editorial offices of *La Revista*, a personal venture started on November 5, 1899, by Julio Herrera y Reissig, the latter decided to come to the defense of the work, and, as a consequence, the young men became acquainted.[9] The influence of De las Carreras on the life of Herrera y Reissig had repercussions on his literary career. Through De las Carreras, who had been in Europe, he was introduced to the works of Albert Samain, and to the most extreme political and social views.

Modernismo in Uruguay was a short and vigorous movement. Through Rubén Darío, or directly from the Decadents, were imported the Black Mass and other elements of Satanism, neurasthenia, absinthe, and the disdain for the average that the Bohemians of Montevideo cultivated in their desire to shock the bourgeois. Their groups disbanded soon, and most of them abandoned the writing of poetry. A few discovered more productive fields in journalism or the theater. Only Julio Herrera y Reissig, in the isolation of his Torre de los Panoramas, continued the exacting task of associating images and rhyming sonnets. His works were usually ignored by the most famous members of the "Generación del 900" of Uruguay. The critic José Enrique Rodó, deploring the extreme disdain for Spanish American life and culture voiced by the Decadents, published no study of Herrera's poetry. Nevertheless, after Herrera's death, Rodó expressed great respect for his talent.[20] Since 1910 the reputation of Herrera y Reissig has increased constantly, and critics and poets of Uruguay are almost unanimous today in their admiration for his poetry.

CHAPTER II

INFLUENCES IN THE WORKS

OF HERRERA Y REISSIG

In the relation of a poet to the historical development that has conditioned his works, the aesthetic position he has inherited, whether consciously expounded or only apparent in his practice, determines the very nature of his writing. When most successful, Herrera y Reissig wrote according to the aesthetic assumptions of the Symbolists.

From La Nouvelle Rive Gauche, in 1882, came the first utterances of one of the many *cénacles* of nineteenth-century Paris. This group was destined to be the source of terms commonly used in discussions of the literature of the times: Decadence and Symbolism. The epithet "decadent" was hurled at Verlaine and his young followers, who took it up as a badge of honor; Verlaine himself had written, in the poem "Langueur," in *Jadis et Naguère* (1884): "Je suis l'Empire à la fin de la décadence." Jean Moréas assembled a group who were first called "les symboliques," and in 1885 he launched the Symbolist school, with manifestoes, banquets, and attendant pomp and circumstance.

There were then three major groups in Paris: the Décadents, gathered around Anatole Baju and his review *Le Décadent*; the Symbolists, around Moréas; and "l'école instrumentiste," under René Ghil, whose name provided an easy rhyme for Verlaine's epigrams. Mallarmé was established in Paris, surrounded by young admirers. His mysterious reputation was later to be enhanced by the promise of *L'Œuvre*. In 1884 he acquired greater prestige when Huysmans praised him, in *À Rebours*, together with Verlaine and Villiers de l'Isle-Adam.

Until 1891 the chaos of manifestoes and schools whirled around these names. At this time Huret's *Enquête* tried, without much success, to clarify the issues. Moréas broke away from Symbolists, Decadents, and all things modern to found his "École romane." Symbolism was represented for a few years by such magazines as *La Plume, L'Ermitage*, and the *Mercure de France*, and by the circle of Mallarmé's personal friends. With his death in 1898 the school ceased to exist as a group, but its fruitful heritage was preserved in the works of Claudel, Gide, Valéry, and other devotees of Mallarmé's "Tuesdays."

The distinction between Symbolists and Decadents is not always easy to determine. If the literary historian chooses to call Decadent the period of French and European letters in which the Decadents were active, the Symbolists become only a group under the common epithet. But the aesthetic tenets of the Symbolists have been traced in a vertical line of succession from Baudelaire, or Poe, to Valéry, passing through Mallarmé. Here the word "Symbolist" is used to describe, not a historical group, but a quality of poetry, a use of aesthetic devices, which has persisted through various periods and has been of great importance in the formative stages of the literature of our time. This concept agrees with the assertion made by Paul Valéry,[1] that Rimbaud and Verlaine continued Baudelaire's pursuit of sensations, while Mallarmé advanced in the road of perfection and purity opened by the master's poetry.

The aesthetic assumptions which Herrera y Reissig inherited from his French sources and from Darío are confused and contradictory. Although never consistently expounded, they were slowly clarified in his poems until, in his most mature poetry, he used the technique of the Symbolists. The way in which this technique was employed in his sonnet series will be discussed in chapter iii. The problems to be studied in the present chapter concern the direct changes produced in the writings of Herrera by his successive acquaintances with other poets.

In the evolution of a poet there may be an abrupt change in themes and even in the use of language that may be traced, by external or internal evidence, to his reading of another poet. In this case we can speak without hesitation of an influence. Two such abrupt changes are found in the works of Herrera. The first occurred in 1900, and is most noticeable in *Las Pascuas del Tiempo*. In this year the poet changed from his youthful writing, in a belatedly Romantic vein, to *modernista* themes and language, mainly as a result of reading Rubén Darío's *Prosas profanas*. The second abrupt change took place in 1903, when several Decadent sonnets by Herrera were published in the June number of the review

Vida Moderna of Montevideo, followed, in August, by "Ciles alucinada," a long poem in sixteen-syllable couplets, dealing with rural themes and characters. In this case the accusation voiced by De las Carreras, that Herrera had Samain "secuestrado en un armario,"[2] and the poet's previous translations from *Aux flancs du vase*, supply the external evidence.

Between 1900 and 1903 Herrera y Reissig was inspired by several French poets who left an imprint on his later work. His early works contain a few reminiscences that clarify the confused problem of his acquaintance with French poetry. These examples will be supplemented, in the discussion of Herrera's poetic evolution, with references to incidental parallels of his themes and lines with earlier poetry in Spanish and French.

Rubén Darío

By 1899 Herrera y Reissig had achieved some local success as a poet. His early attempts are of little value, except as documentary evidence of his development from what he called his "época vergüenza"[3] to more mature writing. They were still in the Romantic vein in vogue in Uruguay before 1895. In spite of the appearance of the *Revista Nacional de Artes y Letras* in that year, Herrera seemed unaware, in his odes to Spain, Castelar, Guido Spano, and his "Canto a Lamartine," of the existence of a new movement. A fragment from "A Guido y Spano" refers to Heine's "Ein Fichtenbaum steht einsam":

> Al vate contemplad! Sin que le importe
> el vil aplauso; a todo indiferente,
> es el pino que Heine pinta en el Norte
> soñando en la palma del Oriente![4]

The poem "La musa de la playa," in the first number of *La Revista*, shows no progress:

> ¡Montevideo, Edén. Ninfa encantada!
> Allá está la ciudad de mis amores,
> Cual desnuda odalisca recostada
> En un diván de espumas y de flores.

This poem contains a reference to Hugo: "El mar es una hipérbole de Hugo."[3] Its commonplace and belated Romanticism represents only the timid attempt of imitative youth. It was published one month before "Wagnerianas,"[4] a Decadent poem in which the influence of Rubén Darío is clear.

The change at this time is most apparent in Herrera's metrical patterns. Without abandoning the hendecasyllable, he tried the twelve-syllable line, the Alexandrine, a sixteen-syllable line with a caesura after the eighth, and unorthodox combinations of different lines: ten and twelve in "Plenilunio," and a daring coupling of eight- and eleven-syllable hemistichs followed by a sixteen-syllable line in "Wagnerianas":

> ¡Oh!, llévame con tus ansias; en las
>   nevadas uvas de tus senos,
> fermenta el vino sublime de los placeres
>   azules.

This experimentation with metrical patterns is clearly the result of his reading of *Prosas profanas*. In Darío he also found new themes to replace the localism of his previous writing. *Modernista* cosmopolitanism runs the gamut of possibilities in *Las Pascuas del Tiempo* (1900). Literary and historical figures are brought together in a festive gathering in which all distinctions are lost: popes and courtesans, Bohemians and moralists, prophets and anarchists, centaurs and queens, mingle freely in a world "de ultratumba."

The decorative elements in the descriptions are
derived from Darío's mythological interests:

> Un buen Término se ríe de un efebo
> que se baña. (p. 38)

This suggests Darío's:

> Reía en su máscara Término barbudo,
> y, como un efebo que fuese una niña.'

The eighteenth-century atmosphere of a superficial
and entertaining Versailles follows Darío's Decadent
tastes:

> Discretos violines hacen historietas
> de pies diminutos, escotes y talles;
> de anillos traidores, de las Antonietas;
> de los galanteos del regio Versalles.
>
> Narran mil alegros, de collares ricos,
> de aleves conquistas, de alcobas doradas,
> las conspiraciones de los abanicos
> y las aventuras de las estocadas.
>
> . . . .
>
> Graves clavicordios, tristes violoncelos.
>   (pp. 44-45)

In these lines the rhythm and the decoration, as well
as the imaginative creation of Versailles, are imitations of one of Darío's most popular poems:

> Era un aire suave, de pausados giros;
> el hada Harmonía ritmaba sus vuelos;
> e iban frases vagas y tenues suspiros
> entre los sollozos de los violoncelos.

Darío's internal rhymes, Wagnerian swan, exotic characters, display of gems and luxuries, worship of France, even the Spanish elements in "Elogio de la seguidilla," are repeated and sometimes travestied:

> Lobengrim y el Cisne. Cadmo transformando
> una piedra (p. 46)
> toma blancas hostias; llueve leve nieve
> (p. 57)
> Entra la Reina de Saba. (p. 39)
> del beso que ritman las formas redondas
> que atesoran opios y magias de Francia.
> (p. 58)
> (Hay espejos, luces, cuadros, pedrería,
> bibelots, Cupidos, oro, mármol, seda ...)
> (p. 47)
> Ríen con la risa del castañeteo,
> Vuelan con el vuelo de la seguidilla. (p. 45)

Ornamental words, made current by Darío's precious tastes, adorn the poem:

> adelfas, orquídeas, lotos y *clemátides*
> . . . .
> ornan los tapices regias *bipsipilas*. (p. 47)

In later works, echoes of Darío's lines, although not so obvious, are found occasionally. Darío's line:

> cual la que pinta Fra Doménico Cavalca.

of "El reino interior," reappears in his disciple, but with a resolutely original tone, in *Los éxtasis de la montaña*:

> Edén que un Fra Doménico soñara en
> acuarelas . . . (p. 165)

Some of the themes which Herrera found in Darío

were to persist in his later work: the eroticism of "Divagación," with its plural exoticism, and the concern with the indifference of women, symbolized in the laughing Eulalia of "Era un aire suave . . . ," are main thematic threads in *Las clepsidras* (1910). The exotic elements of Asia and Africa, originated in France, and the use of figures of Classical mythology were derived from Darío, as well as the French Alexandrine sonnet, which became, after 1904, a favorite pattern in Herrera's poetry.

Baudelaire, Verlaine, Mallarmé

The influence of Baudelaire on the Decadents and the Symbolists was so profound and pervasive that it is impossible to distinguish what elements in the poetry of Herrera come directly from Baudelaire and what elements through some of Baudelaire's French followers or from the Spanish American *modernistas*. Another difficulty arises from the fact that Herrera became acquainted with Edgar Allan Poe in the French poet's translations. He associated the two poets very closely and used their names as symbols of nocturnal despair:

> soy la silenciaria, la de negras alas,
> la trasnochadora que las almas roe,
> la que tiene el brillo de las luces malas
> en que se inspiraron Baudelaire y Poe. (p. 52)

From Poe, Herrera took minor elements. Ulalume became Ulaluma in "La torre de las esfinges," (1909), and the Raven suffered two metamorphoses: a contemplative one, in *Los maitines de la noche* (1902):

> y a lo lejos el cuervo pensativo
> sueña acaso en un Cosmos abstractivo
> como una luna pavorosa y negra; (p. 103)

and, in *Los parques abandonados*, Part II (1908), an elegant raven supplies the background in the epigraph of the sonnet "La alcoba de la agonía":

> Y fué un cuervo galante que visitó mi
> jardín . . . (p. 236)

Although the same symbol as in Poe's poem is used in these two instances, the procedures used by the poets are different. In "The Raven" the whole poem is built around the allegorical figure of the bird. But Herrera's raven has a symbolic and merely suggested meaning which depends on the literary association with Poe's poem.

The influence of Poe on the works of Herrera is only incidental. It came to him through Baudelaire, from whom Herrera took themes and images. In 1900 Herrera made an exceedingly accurate translation of "Une Charogne," but he changed the metrical pattern and the rhyme scheme to a stanza of three Alexandrines and one nine-syllable line, with assonances in the even lines:

> ¿Os recordáis, mi alma, del objeto que vimos
> Esa mañana de verano:
> Al codo de un camino, una carroña infame
> Que estaba sobre un lecho sembrado de
> guijarros?[8]

The themes of "vous serez semblable à cette ordure," and of the persistence of the poet's love after the beloved's death, from "Une Charogne," are both used in the poems "La torre de las esfinges" (1909) and "Berceuse blanca" (1910). The first theme and the description of the decomposition of a cadaver may be related in Baudelaire to Poe's "The

Conqueror Worm." However, it is the second theme that acquires more importance in the poems of Herrera.

The obsession with neurasthenia in Herrera's poetry of the years 1900 to 1903 suggests at times the weakest poems of Baudelaire. The poem "Nivosa" begins with the words, "Es noche de neurastenias," and, in "Desolación absurda," a description of the Decadent fatal woman ends with a reference to Baudelaire:

> ¡Tú eres póstuma y marchita
> misteriosa flor erótica,
> miliunanochesca, hipnótica,
> flor de Estigia ocre y marchita;
> tú eres absurda y maldita,
> desterrada del Placer,
> la paradoja del ser
> en el borrón de la Nada,
> una hurí desesperada
> del harem de Baudelaire!

This same poem opens with a line of "Le Flacon" as an epigraph: "Je serai ton cerceuil, aimable pestilence!"

The Decadent concern with spleen, and its use as a theme and a mood, are of Baudelairean origin, although in the poem "Esplín" the language owes a great deal to Darío:

> Todas las cosas se visten de una vaguedad
>   profunda;
> pálidas nieblas evocan la nostalgia de París;
> hay en el aire perezas de "cocote"
>   meditabunda.
> Llenos están cielo y tierra de un aburrimiento
>   gris.

The ghost of Baudelaire's ennui stalks through the pages of *Los maitines de la noche* (1902), and reappears in "La torre de las esfinges" (1909). Even more important is the Baudelairean theme of guilt, which persists throughout Herrera's career and is dominant in his vision of the world.

Besides the general thematic influence, Herrera appropriated from Baudelaire more detailed elements: the concern with drugs, the obsession with cemeteries and tombs—of Romantic origin, and also common to Mallarmé—elements of Oriental and African exoticism, as well as some traits of Satanism and the technique of passing from the immediate sensuous reality to the evocation of distant worlds. The Baudelairean concern with hashish, although in the manner of Darío, is visible in "Wagnerianas":

>   Quiero libar en tu boca la satánica miel
>   de los venenos:
>   con el haschisch de tus besos me hará ver
>   mil Estambules.

But later, in "Los ojos negros de Julieta," the concern with drugs is much less dependent on Darío's language, and closer to the *paradis artificiels*:

>   alcázares de silencio
>   y Paraísos de opio!

Exotic elements of the Orient are similar in Baudelaire and Herrera. The image "caravanes," as a comparison in "Sed non satiata": "Quand vers toi mes désirs partent en caravanes," may have inspired Herrera's:

>   echóse a descansar, meditabunda,
>   la caravana azul de tus ojeras! . . . (p. 226)

Baudelaire's "langoureuse Asie et . . . brûlante Afrique" are found in the vivid evocations of *Las clepsidras* (1910):

> la Arabia
> lánguida y taciturna de tus ojos (p. 273)

and, in "La torre de las esfinges":

> Canta la noche salvaje
> sus ventriloquias de Congo.

Baudelaire's well-known interest in cats is imitated by Herrera. A cat appears in "La torre de las esfinges" and in the sonnet "El gato," of *Los parques abandonados* (Part II), but it is in "Fiat lux" that Herrera's description parallels Baudelaire most closely:

> Miró el felino con sinuosa línea
> de ópalo.

By means of transferring a quality of the animal's body to its look, Herrera obtained an original result. In this passage he combined lines from two poems, both entitled "Le Chat," of *Les Fleurs du Mal*:

> Ta tête et ton dos élastique
>
> Le feu de ses prunelles pâles,
> Clairs fanaux, vivantes opales.[9]

Another instance of dependence on *Les Fleurs du Mal* is found in the last lines of the sonnet "Supervivencia," which parallel the theme of "Le flambeau vivant":

> Y al inmolarte luz a luz, tus ojos
> sobrevivieron como dos estrellas.

If it is true, as Mallarmé suggests,[10] that this poem of Baudelaire's originated in "To Helen," it would be another indirect influence of Poe.

Herrera took several elements from other Decadents and Symbolists, principally Verlaine, Mallarmé, and Samain; but it is extremely difficult to establish the exact source of his writings, since many of the French poets he read had imitated one another. There are, nevertheless, a few direct references to, and a few clear echoes of, Verlaine. Herrera admired Verlaine and mentions him in "El laurel rosa" (1908), written on the occasion of the death of Sully Prudhomme:

> y Homero y Hugo y Verlaine
> sublimizaron tu nombre.

In *Los parques abandonados* (Part II), a title that suggests Verlaine's "vieux parc solitaire et glacé," Herrera used as an epigraph the lines:

> Je me souviens
> Des jours anciens
>   Et je pleure,

following the title of the sonnet "La ausencia meditativa," which includes an echo of "violons / De l'automne":

> Hoy los pálidos violines
> me anunciaron la agonía de tus últimos
>   jazmines . . .

In the "Poema violeta," of *Las lunas de oro*, the reminiscence is even clearer:

> Mientras lloran los violines
> Amarillos del otoño."[1]

In both the Spanish American poet has added a hypallactic adjective to the original. In the collection *Divagaciones románticas*, one of the least important works of Herrera, the influence of *Fêtes galantes* is noticeable in the choice of subjects and in many secondary elements and reminiscences. Verlaine's desolate parks and his sentimental "clair de lune" are the background of the same vague nostalgias:

> El viejo parque se embruja
> Y se idealiza el canal
>
> Delira un claro de luna
> Entre dos sombras: itú y yo!"²

Unlike the influence of Verlaine, which is incidental and appears mostly in Herrera's minor works, the influence of Mallarmé is deeper. It is an aesthetic influence, the end result of a long development acting on Herrera, rather than the imitation of a procedure. However, a few echoes of Mallarmé's early poetry are noticeable. From one of Mallarmé's most popular poems, "Apparition," comes the "lagrimeo de estrellas" (p. 208), echoing the "Neiger des blancs bouquets d'étoiles." "Fragancia a melancolía"³ parallels Mallarmé's "parfum de tristesse,"⁴ but perhaps through Darío's line, "una fragancia de melancolía," in "Yo soy aquel . . ."

The sonnet "Solo verde-amarillo para flauta, llave de U," bears the epigraph, "Manera de Mallarmé," but has no thematic relation to Mallarmé's poetry. It does, however, imitate Mallarmé's attempt to produce musical effects by the repetition of sounds. This sonnet plays on "u" sounds, as "Le pitre châtié" of Mallarmé does on the sounds of "é," "ai," "è," and so on:

SOLO VERDE-AMARILLO PARA FLAUTA,
LLAVE DE U.

> Virgilio es amarillo
> y Fray Luis verde.
> (Manera de Mallarmé)

(Andante)
> Ursula punza la boyuna yunta;
> la'lujuria perfuma con su fruta,
> la púbera frescura de la ruta
> por donde ondula la venusa junta.

>   (*Piano*)
>   Recién la hirsuta barba rubia apunta
>   al dios Agricultura. La impoluta (*Pianissimo*)
>   uña fecunda del amor, debuta
>
>   (*Crescendo*)
>   cual una duda de nupcial pregunta.
>   Anuncian lluvias las adustas lunas.
>   Almizcladuras, uvas, aceitunas,
>
>   (*Forte*)
>   gulas de mar, fortunas de las musas;
>
>   (*Fortissimo*)
>   han madurado todas las verduras.
>   Hay bilis en las rudas armaduras;
>   y una burra hace hablar las cornamusas.

A similar relationship can be established between the poem "Amor épico" and Mallarmé's sonnet "Le vierge, le vivace et le bel aujourd'hui." Herrera repeated the vowel "i," in the accented position at the end of the line, as the French poet did. The "éventails"—"en el país de tu abanico negro" (p. 218)—and the symbolical amazons, in the poem "Amazona" of *Las clepsidras*, recall some of Mallarmé's favorite images.

Albert Samain

Samain, a late Symbolist who was once fashionable and greatly admired in the Spanish world, but is no longer considered a great poet, popularized many Decadent themes. The suggestive and ethereal world of Symbolist creation was made more accessible through his sentimental treatment. Although he was a disciple of Mallarmé, he followed Verlaine also,

and his Symbolism is consequently of a hybrid nature—
to such a point that the Danish critic Svend Johansen
maintains that Samain is not a Symbolist."[15] Samain's
poems had already been introduced into the River
Plate region. His influence is noticeable in the work
of Leopoldo Lugones, a few of whose poems were
known to Herrera before 1900. The priority of Lugones
in the adaptation to Spanish of the Decadent themes
of Samain has been established,[16] although for a few
years it was a matter of local controversy.

The influence of Samain on Herrera, which was to
last throughout his literary life, began in 1900, as a
result of his translations from *Aux flancs du vase*.
From 1900 to 1903, a period of metrical experimentation for Herrera, the influence of Samain was secondary, manifested mainly in a predilection for the color
"violeta," and such words as "heliotropos" and
"amatistas." After 1903 his use of rural themes
reveals a deliberate decision to continue in the
footsteps of Samain. In "Ciles alucinada" (1903), the
two collections *Los éxtasis de la montaña* (Part I,
1904, Part II of uncertain date), and *Sonetos vascos*
(1906), the thematic influence is most noticeable, and
it reappears, though sporadically, in the second part
of *Los parques abandonados* (1908).

Aux flancs du vase was, for Herrera, the vehicle
of a late nineteenth-century tendency: a renewed
interest in the pastoral convention, which had been
nearly abandoned in the first decades of the century.
Herrera seems not to have known Tennyson's *Idylls
of the King* (1858) or Laprade's *Idylles héroïques*
(1859)—books that started the trend—or Henri de
Régnier's *Jeux rustiques et divins* (1897) or the
early works of Francis Jammes. As a result of the
influence of Samain and of Rubén Darío, Herrera
wrote several series of Alexandrine sonnets on rural
themes.

In regard to the Shakespearean sonnet, T. S. Eliot has pointed out that to adapt and create a pattern in the poetry of a language is not merely to incorporate a new metrical scheme. It is also to appropriate the rhythm, moods, and emotions of the original. The Alexandrine sonnet, one of many contributions of *modernismo* to Spanish poetry, should, like the Shakespearean sonnet, be considered "not merely such-and-such a pattern, but a precise way of thinking and feeling."[7] Rubén Darío had imported this pattern from the French, unaware of the Spanish antecedent, and his *modernista* disciples followed him. The adaptation was a collective undertaking, in which the sonnets of Herrera y Reissig were of importance because of his persistent and masterly use of the pattern, which acquired a new flexibility in his hands.

Herrera's dependence on Darío rather than on Samain is clearly proved by the fact that, in his translations, Herrera did not use the Alexandrine, but a sixteen-syllable line with a caesura after the eighth—really a double octosyllable—the same line he was to use in his first poem on a rural theme, "Ciles alucinada." Apart from this change, and a different position of the rhymes, his translations are extremely faithful to the original. For this very reason, the few deviations found in them reveal Herrera's originality. They usually turn the sentimental and vague picture of Samain's poetry into a more distinct image. One of his most successful renderings, "Myrtil et Palémone," follows the French poem closely:

> Myrtil et Palémone, enfants chers aux bergers,
> Se poursuivent dans l'herbe épaisse des vergers,
> Et font fuir devant eux, en de bruyantes joies,
> La file solennelle et stupide des oies.
> Or Myrtil a vaincu Palémone en ses jeux;

Comme il l'étreint, rieuse, entre ses bras
    fougueux,
Il frémit de sentir, sous les toiles légères,
Palpiter tout à coup des formes étrangères;
Et la double rondeur naissante des seins
    nus
Jaillit comme un beau fruit sous ses doigts
    ingénus.
Le jeu cesse . . . Un mystère en son cœur
    vient d'éclore,
Et, grave, il les caresse et les caresse
    encore.

Palémone y Myrtil, niños amados de los
    pastores,
Se persiguen en los huertos entre el
    césped abundante,
Y con júbilos ruidosos, hacen huir, por
    delante,
La fila grave y estúpida de los gansos
    roncadores.
A Palémone, Myrtil ha vencido con sus
    mañas;
Y al estrecharla, risueña, entre sus brazos
    amantes,
Tiembla de pronto, al sentir tras las telas
    palpitantes,
Cabe su pecho el latido dulce de formas
    extrañas . . .
Y la doble redondez del blanco seno en
    botón
Brota como un bello fruto bajo la ingenua
    caricia.
El juego cesa , . . Un misterio despunta en
    su corazón
Y, él, grave, los acaricia y siempre los
    acaricia.

In this translation, which follows the original poem with such fidelity, the few unavoidable departures are due mostly to the necessities of meter and rhyme, but the addition of the adjective "roncadores" in line four seems to bring to the poem a quality which is characteristic of Herrera's own poetry: the use of homely vocabulary in an attempt to raise the prosaic reality of village life to the level of poetic wonder. In the same way the line,

> Et puis ferme la porte et chasse les abeilles,

in "Le repas préparé," is rendered,

> Y luego espanta las moscas después de
> cerrar la puerta.

The familiar flies are more likely to be found in a dining room. This attachment to the homely was not necessary, since Herrera could have kept the original "abejas," by suppressing the conjunction "y."

Many of the episodes of the collection which Herrera had partially translated found their way later into the village world of his own poems. In "Ciles alucinada," the ecstacy of the young Ciles is a development of Hermione's experience in "Hermione et les Bergers":

> Un mystère autour d'elle a transformé les
> choses,
> Doux comme un flot de lune en été sur des
> roses.

The description of a happy family gathering, in "La velada," derives from such poems as "Le repas préparé," "Niza chante," and "Le bonheur," and the simple love story of "Amphise et Melitta" is repeated by Edipo and Diana. The lines:

Ah, bañarse en la atómica desnudez de
   las cosas
y morir en los brazos de la buena Cibeles!
   (p. 159)

of "El dintel de la vida," in the second part of *Los éxtasis de la montaña*, follow Samain's vague "être universel." The peasant flutes, the lamb as a symbol of innocence, and the Greek names have also been translated into Herrera's sonnets.

Many of the interests and decorative elements in the poetry of Herrera come from *Au jardin de l'infante* and *Le Chariot d'or*. Schumann's name, the melancholy evening train, are Samainian in origin. Herrera was so familiar with the French poet's language that he borrowed expressions and mannerisms: "Couleur de songe," for instance, was used as the title of a poem, "Color de sueño." The "plaine, au loin déserte, pense" became, in Herrera's more graphic phrase "La arruga pensativa que tiene la montaña." Sometimes exact counterparts of Samain's rural characters are found in the sonnets of *Los éxtasis de la montaña*: "el astrónomo, el vate y el mentor" are derived from Damoetas and Methymne, and the Astronomer in "La cátedra" reproduces Clydès from "La Sagesse."[1]

The Spanish American poet, however, while using Samain's themes, created an independent and forceful poetic world. The distinctive traits of Herrera's lines become apparent when we compare the poems in *Los éxtasis de la montaña* that parallel Samain's most closely. "Xanthis" and "El baño"[19] deal with similar situations, both preceded by Mallarmé's "L'Après-midi d'un faune." In "Xanthis" a bathing beauty discovers that a satyr has been watching her; in "El baño" three bathing shepherdesses are stealthily watched by three shepherds. Samain delights in the description of the girl:

> Le flot de ses cheveux d'un seul côté
>   s'épanche,
> Et, blanche, elle sourit à son image
>   blanche . . .
> Elle admire sa taille droite, ses beaux
>   bras,
> Et sa hanche polie, et ses seins délicats.

Herrera's poem deviates from "Xanthis" in two opposite directions: it paints a more authentic picture of rural life, replacing the satyr with three swains; also, it proceeds to a more general interpretation of nature, in a projection of erotic desires into the ripples of the lake. Samain's description is static; Herrera's scene is presented dynamically, through the use of motor images and verbs of movement. The sonnet is built in a dynamic line that reconstructs the scene and the movements of the shepherdesses— from their home to a lake—and of swains in shame-faced flight:

> Entre sauces que velan una anciana casuca,
> donde se desvistieron devorando la risa,
> hacia el lago, Foloe, Safo, y Ceres, de prisa
> se adelantan en medio de la tarde caduca.
>
> Atreve un pie Foloe, bautízase la nuca
> y ante el espejo de ámbar arróbase indecisa;
> meneando el talle, Safo respinga su camisa
> y corre, mientras Ceres gatea y se
>   acurruca . . .
>
> Después de agrias posturas y esperezos
>   felinos,
> gimiendo un ¡ay! glorioso se abrazan a las
>   ondas,
> que críspanse con lúbricos espasmos
>   masculinos . . .

> Mientras, ante el misterio de sus gracias
>   redondas,
> Loth, Febo y David, púdicos tanto como
>   ladinos,
> las contemplan y pálidos huyen entre las
>   frondas.

The poems "Le Laboureur" and "El labrador" exemplify another fundamental difference between the poets. Besides changing from a vague and sentimental description to precision in the portrayal of a character and intensity of emotion, Herrera shows a concern with moral qualities and defects that is never found in the poetry of his French model. It is this concern that made it necessary for Herrera to resort to irony and humor—absent from Samain's poetry—in the creation of his rural world.

CHAPTER III

FROM IMAGE TO MYTH

THE IMPASSE OF SYMBOLISM

Through Baudelaire's translations and interpretations, the French Symbolists inherited from Edgar Allan Poe some conceptions and beliefs of the Romantic era. The sentimental cosmology of the essay "Eureka," translated in 1859, found its way into the poetics of Baudelaire, who projected his own personality into Poe's works and took freely from them. He seized upon the ideas expounded by Poe and turned them into a program of poetry. The alternately contracting and expanding universe of Poe's theory was accepted, together with the final identification of the individual and the universe. "Et maintenant, ce cœur divin,—quel est-il? *C'est notre propre cœur,*"¹ asserted the master.

The antipositivist reaction at the turn of the century took refuge in various doctrines of the occult, and found pseudomystical metaphysics to its taste. "Eureka" was preferred precisely because it was less systematic and more daring than many speculations on nature of the early nineteenth century. Through the Symbolists, vague and distorted monistic conceptions were diffused abroad. And Herrera learned from Samain and others the cosmological doubts and revelations of a weary and nervous *fin de siècle*. His *personae* reproduced the poet's pseudomystic experiences. Ciles, in the first of Herrera's poems on rural themes, is saved from the confused suffering of her jealousy and disillusionment by just such a reverie:

> Repentino languidece. Una infinita delicia
> la invade; todo su pecho se dilata a una
>   caricia
> de ingenuas aspiraciones. Aquiétase . . .
>   El magnetismo
> de su lacónica patria, y un oscuro panteísmo
> que no comprende, la postran. (p. 121)

Herrera uttered the despair and pessimism of his "misantropía" through his masks. As a rescuing force, compenetration with the All brings final acceptance of universal laws. The episodes in which the poet records the progress of a mind toward purgation are reproduced through images. His thoughts and emotions have been projected into fragmentary successions of impressionistic pictures. It could be said of Herrera, as Thibaudet has said of Mallarmé, that he was "la victime du discontinu."² Herrera was not able to organize his creation into a unified whole, and relied, in his mythopeic efforts, on the suggestion provided by the momentary and the vivid.

The Image in Herrera's Poetry

Poetry, when trying to avoid logical discourse, tends to an excessive dependence on sensorial representation. Through images which in themselves carry no meaning, the Symbolist poet suggests his emotional state and conveys his understanding of nature. It is his task to create a system of coördinates with a complete existence. The third dimension—the one which is to awaken in the reader the response parallel to the poet's experience—is the power of suggestion that supplies the depth in an otherwise two-dimensional world. The suggestive power of an image, when incorporated into a context, can radiate and penetrate the several spheres of meaning necessary in the creation of a symbol. This system of coördinates may be used to explain the significance of natural phenomena.

In Herrera's transposition of the phenomenal world, the kinetic sense is resorted to most successfully. The texture of his lines is, however, extremely varied, with much shifting from one sense to another in scintillating rapidity:

> Cien fugas de agua viva rezan a la discreta
> ventura de los campos sin lábaro y sin
>   tronos.
> El incienso sulfúrico que arde por los
>   abonos
> se hermana a los salobres yodos de la
>   caleta . . . (p. 184)

There is no logical statement of the significance of a scene. Colors are spread over the canvas rather than restricted to definite shapes; movements and feelings are projected into inanimate objects and animals. Herrera's poems present an animistic nature, personified in vivid pictures. Even abstract qualities acquire movement and life:

> La inocencia del día se lava en la fontana.

The visual-kinetic image in this line does not reproduce the world as it is believed to be, but creates a hypothetical existence, independent of, and only subtly related to, a possible dawn. The reality thus transposed exists only in itself, and is subject only to forces and laws within a magnetic field of its own:

> Y hacia la aurora sesgan agudas golondrinas
> como flechas perdidas de la noche en derrota.

In Herrera's new vision, the elements of the static, conventional world are freely endowed with characteristics of other spheres of being:

> Llovió. Trisca a lo lejos un sol convaleciente.
>   (p. 148)
> Rebota en los collados la grita rutinaria.
>   (p. 150)
> Rasca un grillo el silencio perfumado de
>   rosas . . . (p. 175)

An animal movement lends its vivacity to the sun, human sounds have the physical qualities of rubber balls, and a purposeful action transforms the nocturnal cricket. This combination of sensorial impressions and forces from different realms, in apparent disorder, is a tool of rearrangement and creation. The exuberance and complexity of the natural world is paralleled in Herrera's poetry by his use of images of different orders: olfactory, gustative, thermic, tactile, and kinesthetic:

y se exhaló de tu vestido un franco
efluvio de alhucema y de vainilla (p. 227)

Afuera el aire es plomo . . . (p. 187)

La emoción del crepúsculo pesa solemnemente
 (p. 177)

Una música absurda y poseída
con cárdeno sabor de sepultura (p. 225)

From this wealth of sensorial impressions, complexes of a synaesthetic quality frequently develop. Their function in the poem is closely related to the poet's conception of an animistic nature, and his desire to allude to a different reality through their suggestiveness.

Synaesthetic Images

Combinations of images of different categories are based on the psychological phenomenon called synaesthesia, which may occur as an experience of normal life but is more frequent under the influence of narcotics. Certainly the phenomenon itself has no aesthetic value, nor is there any value inherent in the combined evocation the poet may create by reproducing two or three different sensations associated with a single stimulus. The interest of nineteenth-century poets in synaesthesia led to extravagances now forgotten: the alcoholic symphonies of Des Esseintes and René Ghil's theories and tables of the exact relationships of sounds, perfumes, colors, and feelings are exaggerations of the trend. Nevertheless, the serious efforts which followed the programmatic sonnet "Correspondances" were basic in the evolution of French Symbolism and in the writings of Herrera y Reissig.

"Correspondances" was the vehicle through which the Symbolists became concerned with a phenomenon which had been observed sporadically since the eighteenth century:

> La Nature est un temple où de vivants piliers
> Laissent parfois sortir de confuses paroles;
> L'homme y passe à travers des forêts de symboles
> Qui l'observent avec des regards familiers.
>
> Comme de longs échos qui de loin se confondent
> Dans une ténébreuse et profonde unité,
> Vaste comme la nuit et comme la clarté,
> Les parfums, les couleurs et les sons se répondent.
> Il est des parfums frais comme des chairs d'enfants,
> Doux comme les hautbois, verts comme les prairies,
> —Et d'autres, corrompus, riches et triomphants,
>
> Ayant l'expansion des choses infinies,
> Comme l'ambre, le musc, le benjoin et l'encens,
> Qui chantent les transports de l'esprit et des sens.

Based on the analogies of sensorial experience and a hidden reality, a theory of the symbol is advanced in the quatrains. The "ténébreuse et profonde unité" is accessible through the perfumes, colors, and sounds which are the signs of, and clues to, the mystery. The eighth line defines the relationship between sounds, colors, and perfumes, which is presented in detail in the sestet. The last lines continue the exploration of a method of poetic knowledge with illustrations of the kind of synaesthetic experiences to which the poet, in Baudelaire's conception, should attend.

The anticlimactic sestet complements the theory of the symbol with a theory of synaesthesia, the function of which is to express the intuitions of the "esprit" through concrete analogies supplied by the senses. In the poem "La Chevelure," the theory expounded here is put into practice with the evocation, through a perfume, of a vision of distant beauty. This procedure was followed by Baudelaire's disciples in directions which were congenial to their own temperaments: some accentuated his fondness for complicated and luxurious images; some resorted to the phenomenon sparingly and only as a secondary device.

Herrera's use of synaesthesia developed from an early reliance on strangeness for decorative effect to its use, in his mature poetry, as an introduction to a hallucinatory world. A line of the early poem *Las Pascuas del Tiempo* contains a combination of color and sound:

> los himnos más rojos en tono i bemol. (p. 44)

Obviously, in the poet's explanation of the universal text, this line does not contain that "confuse parole" which may illuminate the road to "darkness" and "profound unity." But the synaesthesia in Herrera's late work opens up vistas of further significance:

> Ardió el epitalamio de tu paso
> un himno de trompetas fulgurantes . . .
>   (p. 276)

Sometimes the synaesthesia consists only of the bare statement that a sensation of one category suggests another. This is the simplest representation of the psychological phenomenon and, although it may acquire great beauty as a decorative element, it is seldom the central pivot in Herrera's poetry. In the two following examples there are incidental associations of olfactory and visual sensations:

> Frufrutó de aventura tu aéreo traje,
> sugestivo de aromas y de espliego ...
> (p. 232)

> un cántico de arpegios tan sencillos
> que hablaban de romeros y de hinojos.
> (p. 199)

More frequently, synaesthesia is represented by several sensations incorporated into one indissoluble unit, which may become central in the poem and supply the reader with a mythical transcription of nature:

> El sol es miel, la brisa pluma y el cielo
> pana ... (p. 158)

The aesthetic effect thus produced is frequently combined in Symbolist poetry with the use of hypallactic adjectives. Hypallages of a simple kind, in which an adjective logically related to one term is transferred to another in the same sentence, and also elliptic hypallages, in which the real term of reference for the adjective is not expressed, are common in Herrera's poetry. In the following example, the adjective "flébil" belongs grammatically with "cabeza," but it is transferred to the abstract noun "devoción":

> la flébil devoción de tu cabeza (p. 201)

In the next lines the real term of reference for the adjective "procaces" is not expressed:

> de procaces sulfatos una impura
> fragancia conspiraba a nuestro paso (p. 204)

The result is an unusual entity of more dreadful significance than the real one might be.

The combination of a hypallage and a reference to a sensation constitutes a special case of synaesthesia. Symbolist poets have created lines of rare beauty by means of this figure, as in Mallarmé's "Salut":

> Le blanc souci de notre toile.

The hypallage is especially frequent in the poetry of Maeterlinck. Examples are abundant in the poetry of Herrera:

> Citándonos, después de oscura ausencia
> (p. 198)
>
> El áspero responso de tu olvido. (p. 206)

In the second of these lines, in which a tactile adjective is added to an auditive image, although it belongs with the noun "olvido," the poetic effect is probably heightened by the association with, or a reminiscence of, Garcilaso's hendecasyllable:

> Por la oscura región de vuestro olvido.

Synaesthetic hypallages that add a color to an abstract noun, a figure known as "ethical color," are found in Herrera's later poetry:

> Y en tu collar de rojos sacrilegios. (p. 277)

Because of this concern with images and their function in poetry—of which figures of speech are only signs—the Symbolists tended to ignore all other possibilities of expression. They concentrated on the intensification of the evocative value of their lines. In Herrera this obsession with one manner of expression often produced a poem overwrought with sensuous luxury, a fact which has at times resulted in critical misinterpretation of his works. The last of his sonnet collections, *Las clepsidras*, has been considered only "una orgía de decoración,"[3] under the brilliance of which it is impossible to find any meaning.[4]

Symbol and Myth

In their aesthetic writing the Symbolists resorted constantly and confusedly to the term "symbol." For them it meant a great many things, from the mystical sign of a cognitive process—a key to the universal analogies—to the work of art itself. Out of the confusion in aesthetic thinking among French writers of the latter part of the century, the term "symbol" has survived, to designate the technical unit in the poetry of a group that followed Mallarmé. Since they considered that the image had power to convey the poetic experience, it can be assumed that the image is the primary constituent of a symbol. The definition of "symbol" can be more clearly understood if the problem is posed indirectly as an inquiry into the peculiar circumstances that transform an image into a symbol.

Evidently this transformation can occur only within the poem, and it is in some way related to the acclimatization of the image within the whole—an acclimatization effected through its power of suggestion, which relates it to other words within a context. If for instance, "lamb" means "purity," it is idle to substitute "lamb" for the concept "purity" unless the word "lamb" contains elements that add to the direct identification and make this substitution a gain. These elements are relationships with other concretions of meaning in the poem and in the language of the poet's tradition. In a poetry which accomplishes the task of expression through images, the symbol is "l'expression suggestive d'une tonalité dans une image qui contient la possibilité d'une transcendance multiple." In this definition, "tonalité" is the diffuse state of poetic precreation, the unnamed *x* the poet pursues in concentric circles of gradual approximation. This *x* exists within the realization of the symbol: "Le symbole et l'absence sont le même processus, vu simplement de deux points de vue différents."[8]

Existing only within a context, the symbol, as understood here, is always an aesthetic unit. It may be of greater or lesser value as poetry, but it always has form and unity. Part of its essence is to transcend the boundaries of the circle sensation-image and become an interpretation of natural phenomena, a myth. Not all myths are expressed through symbols, however. In a certain sense, the interpretations of natural phenomena offered by science are myths translated into abstract formulas, and the formulas here are symbols only in the general sense of the word. They are signs, but not image-symbols of the kind used by the poets under discussion.

It may be clearer now why the Symbolists, and Herrera y Reissig as a follower of the movement in Spanish America, resorted to synaesthesia with great frequency and at times with almost blind faith. They used the identification of two sensations of different order as an allusion to the existence of a third order. The synaesthesia was then a signpost of "dérèglement," and also a gateway to the "absent life." It seemed to them that, because of its complexity, a synaesthetic image was by its very nature more appropriate to the creation of the symbol. They rashly dismissed all art that did not proceed according to their own technique of concatenation of images. Some of their later exegetes have repeated, in this respect, their condemnation of the allegory.

The works of a Symbolist need to be viewed as a whole. In fact, the very obsession of the Symbolist poet with the suggestive power of words has led him into a search so subtle that only by retracing every step of his long journey can we reproduce the structure of meanings which he himself saw in a single one of his poems. Totality in his works is a product of condensation, within the limits of a poem, of the sum total of associations and emotional repercussions which the outside world has produced in a mind "placé devant l'extérieur, non pas comme devant un spectacle, ou comme un thème à devoirs français, mais comme devant un texte, avec cette question: *Qu'est-ce que ça veut dire?*"[6] Hence Mallarmé's followers were expecting a poem, *L'Oeuvre*, which should contain, in its unity, the totality of all suggestions. Yet, when the poet deals with sensations, the momentary always triumphs, and the result is always partial. If, at a given time, the poet has experienced the sensations produced by a "special, rural scene," either actually or in his imagination, he tends to reproduce the visual-kinetic picture of the early morning and the end of night. The result is an independent dynamic unit of contrasting forces:

La inocencia del día se lava en la fontana

Y hacia la aurora sesgan agudas golondrinas
como flechas perdidas de la noche en derrota.

These lines are examples of the perfect sequences of words which Valéry's Goddess of the Continuum[7] sings to tempt poets away from the safety of silence into the crime of poetry—sequences which haunted the Symbolists and were called "*vers incantatoires*." They contain two images that are the poles around which the poem revolves:

 EL DESPERTAR .

Alisa y Cloris abren de par en par la puerta
y torpes con el dorso de la mano haragana,

restréganse los húmedos ojos de lumbre
   incierta,
por donde huyen los últimos sueños de
   la mañana . . .

La inocencia del día se lava en la fontana,
el arado en el surco vagaroso despierta,
y en torno de la casa rectoral, la sotana
del cura se pasea gravemente en la huerta . . .

Todo suspira y ríe. La placidez remota
de la montaña sueña celestiales rutinas.
El esquilón repite siempre su misma nota

de grillo de las cándidas églogas matutinas.
Y hacia la aurora sesgan agudas golondrinas
como flechas perdidas de la noche en derrota.

The first quatrain presents in rapid succession a series of movements—"abren," "restréganse," "huyen"—culminating in the all-inclusive movement of the fifth line. This line, when considered in the context, becomes a symbol and contains the preceding movements and a personal interpretation of natural phenomena. In it the poet expresses only his own private vision of the poetic essence of the morning. Hence the difficulty of Symbolist poetry: it is not only a difficulty of understanding, of supplying missing logical links, or of unraveling the skein of unorthodox syntax, but also an absolute difficulty, occurring, as in this poem, even when the lines themselves seem perfectly clear to the eye of the casual reader.

This difficulty is due to the impossibility of recapturing the poet's experience. A Symbolist is never willing to explain and clarify. But clues are often given by which the meaning can be disentangled. In "El despertar," lines eleven and twelve offer an unmistakable explanation, preceded by a few descriptive metaphors that continue the animistic vision of objects. Plow, cassock, and mountain are endowed with movement and feelings. In the *pars pro toto*, "la sotana del cura se pasea," there is an undertone of playful humor that results from the euphoric attitude of the observer, and, when the ingenuous life of the moment is finally expressed, the reader accepts the bell as the register in which man jots down the naïveté of morning eclogues. This sonnet is an expression of the theme of innocence, a major interest in the poetry of Herrera.

The poet has succeeded here in creating a mythical interpretation of reality—his task of private expression. The reader is left to fend for himself, and whether he can reproduce the poet's experience is of no consequence. One of the peculiar characteristics of Symbolist poetry is this absolute disregard for the language of the tribe and for the public function of art. The Symbolist poet lives in fear of being understood. He is concerned with the personal, the exquisite, and the different; he shuns the facile accomplishment of communal language. As a result, his output is limited. The road of the personal is the road to unintelligibility and impotence.

Private Myth and Community Myth

The aesthetic position which Herrera inherited from the Symbolists exacted the expression of the personal against the communicative value of words. Mallarmé's *Un Coup de dés* borders on incommunicability and typifies the extreme of Symbolist esotericism. A late development of the Romantic concept of originality had been carried to an extreme and revolt was necessary. In Mallarmé himself we can find both the extreme and the revolt: on the one hand, the typographical arrangement, the personal *mise en page*,[1] with its recondite meanings, exemplifies an aberrant extreme of originality; on the other hand, the figure of "Le Maître" in *Un Coup de dés*, although an original creation, seems to have been intended as a general myth to be adopted by the community of those who speak the same language. Other Symbolists, anticipated by Mallarmé's *Hérodiade*, resorted to myths of longer standing, as witness Valéry's *Narcisse*, in an effort at communication.

In the last poems of Herrera's career we sense a new direction, perhaps the result of dissatisfaction with the limitations of the private myth. This dissatisfaction is characteristic of late developments in Symbolism. The contradictory necessity for an understanding public drove the Symbolist poets, paradoxically, to attempts at reintegrating the historical myths of the race. They tried to create a new vision by associating the mythologies of the past with the life of the present.

Herrera must have felt that his own art was becoming less communicable. His cold reception by the reading public must have warned him that he was entering the region of absolute hermeticism and that "something taken up and constructed from a tradition will be accessible to others enjoying that tradition; with the corollary that an incommunicable utterance is a bad utterance and not worth troubling about.'" The conflict between expression and communication is apparent in Herrera's attempts at self-exegesis: extensive footnoting in "La vida" (written before 1904), explanatory subtitles in his collections, and epigraphs to separate poems.

As a result of this conflict, Herrera finally turned to myths sanctioned by community traditions. "La muerte del pastor" (1907) is centered in the symbol of *la carreta*, still of the nature of the private myth. The fact that the cart is to come no longer is repeatedly referred to as the sign of the shepherd's death. But at the end of the poem the "carreta" appears as a ghost cart in the imaginations of the inhabitants of the rural community, in this way providing a communal belief for a private myth.

Herrera's most important attempts at communicability are, paradoxically, in works that have been considered least intelligible: "La torre de las esfinges" (1909) and *Las clepsidras* (1910). In the first, a poem that has been a source of scandal in the criticism of his work,[10] Oedipus is the central unifying character, equivalent to Mallarmé's "Le Maître" in *Un Coup de dés*, a poem Herrera did not know. Besides this Classical myth, the poem resorts to parallel literary and legendary allusions to express the emotion of guilt. In *Las clepsidras*, Herrera "summoned myths from widely separated periods and places to find in them a common element."[11] This telescoping of myths in order to create a new reality developed from the Symbolists. It was a major preoccupation in the writings of Herrera y Reissig, although he seldom succeeded in organizing his fragments into a whole.

CHAPTER IV

THE EARLY POEMS OF

HERRERA Y REISSIG

Before Herrera y Reissig succeeded in assimilating Symbolist aesthetics, his works often intimated the concerns and themes that were to persist in his sonnet collections. His pseudophilosophical and allegorical poems, especially, provide a clue to his later writings. In his apprenticeship in the literature of the late nineteenth century, the variety of attempts, the contradictory interests, and the numerous directions of Herrera's beginnings testify, though not yet to the rise of a new idiom, to his restlessness and ambition. He had to try many patterns and adopt and discard the clichés in vogue before he could find and

develop his own diction. The precious tastes of
Rubén Darío had to be contrasted with a homely
vocabulary to reproduce his own struggle with the
language. His preparatory efforts, *Los maitines de
la noche* (1902) and "Ciles alucinada" (1903), are
the most striking examples of his early manner; after
this there is an obvious change in his poetry.

Herrera's writings before 1904 were often imitative,
but at times suggest his later mastery. Still couched
in Romantic language and imitating the novel rhythms
introduced by Darío, "El hada Manzana" (1900) is
a clumsy allegorical piece, far from his later Symbolist
technique. Nor do the emblematical characters of the
philosophical poem "La vida" have any life as they
strive to chart the voyage of a mind in search of the
unknowable.

The longest and most pretentious poem of the
youthful Herrera, *Las Pascuas del Tiempo* (1900),
brings together the personages of history and mythology and conducts the reader through a vast and
exotic world, the whole presided over by the unifying
figure of "Time," which is described in a refrain
obviously modeled after Darío in rhythm, décor, and
choice of words:

> El Viejo Patriarca,
> que todo lo abarca,
> se riza la barba de príncipe asirio;
> su nívea cabeza parece un gran lirio,
> parece un gran lirio la nívea cabeza del
>   viejo Patriarca. (p. 37)

The poem expresses delight in the discovery of the
world of culture—a discovery that was part of the
Zeitgeist of the continent at the turn of the century,
when Spanish American writers were devoting their
creative effort to a poetry "de cultura,"[1] of which
Las Pascuas del Tiempo is only one of many examples.

The joyful innocence of some passages of "Ciles

alucinada" contrasts with the strained poetry of *Los maitines de la noche*, in which the jangling line expresses the nervousness of modern spleen, neurasthenia, guilt, and remorse. Here, for the first time, Herrera's concern with the problem of good and evil becomes evident. In him, as in the French Decadents, the paraphernalia of Satanism very often produced the morbid tones and the blasphemous pose in fashion since the Romantics. Yet, after a superficial interest in the Black Mass and demonology, Herrera slowly evolved—under the influence of Baudelaire—a deep concern for moral problems. This is clear in a fragment of his usually confused prose: "Conviene que el sufrimiento y la injusticia y el crimen y la desigualdad existan. El mal es una condición del bien, como no su agente lógico."[1]

Henceforth the poet's aim was to interpret a cosmos in which the conflict of good and evil, of innocence and guilt, is central. His artistic vision thereby gained the depth and intensity that set it apart from the poetry written in Uruguay before him. The problems of the origin of evil in the universe, of sexual guilt and infidelity in love, of unchecked greed, are explored through age-old myths and through the actions and sufferings of Herrera's characters. However, the morbid fashions of late nineteenth-century literature are often apparent in Herrera's dissonant swing from extreme to extreme, and it is only in his best moments that he created the moral portrait of a character.

Los maitines de la noche

The miscellaneous poems in this collection were written between 1900 and 1902, with some later additions. Herrera seems not to have been concerned yet with the orderly grouping of his poems. Later he proceeded to arrange them in unified books and to define the central interest of his collections in explanatory subtitles. In *Los maitines de la noche* he continued to experiment with metrical patterns, and tried, for the first time, the sonnet and the *décima*. These two traditional patterns were to be his favorite, and almost exclusive, rhythms, after 1904. Among the least valuable poems in this early book, "Esplín," "Nivosa," "Wagnerianas," and other immature poems imitate the nervous dissonances and morbid currents of nineteenth-century verse. Besides these poems of loose metrical pattern, the collection includes sonnets, some of which relate sentimental stories by indirection: "Alba triste" is an episode of infidelity;[3] "La vejez prematura," the emotional distress of love coming to an end; "El desamparo," a story of seduction. Other sonnets—"Enero," "Mayo," "Julio," and "Octubre"—interpret the seasons of the Southern Hemisphere through reference to distant lands.

The Oriental exoticism of Herrera's earlier writings supplies the decoration in some passages, but the evocation is more successful than it had been in the halting lines of previous poems. Now one stroke suffices to bring to mind a variety of sensations from an unreal geography:

> Una encantada Estambul
> surge de tu guardapelo. (p. 91)

"Desolación absurda" marks the beginning of a complex interpretation of natural reality through a projection into inanimate objects of human intentions and the consciousness of mental activity. The descriptions reveal progress in conciseness and the exact use of words. At times, the purposelessness of human games illuminates the playful irresponsibility of immediate phenomena:

> y los sauces en montón
> obseden los camalotes

> como torvos hugonotes
> de una muda emigración.
> . . . .
> Juega el viento perfumado,
> con los pétalos que arranca
> una partida muy blanca
> de un ajedrez perfumado.

The poet resorts also to works of art, manufactured articles, and even punctuation marks as frames of reference and comparison, in an effort to minimize the vastness of nature and make it more intelligible. Emotions are reproduced in images apparently of little importance, as in the final lines of "Desolación absurda," which suggest Góngora's "paréntesis frondosos / al período son de su corriente":

> Yo te abriré con mis brazos
> un paréntesis de amor.

The poems contain a few descriptive fragments of rural landscapes, and a deftly sketched shepherdess makes sudden appearances:

> una zagala brinca en el sendero (p. 103)

> Una pastora me contaba el caso
> del novio que le tuvo más apego:
> un inocente corderito ciego
> que no alcanzó a vivir un año escaso. (p. 106)

These echoes of the poet's reading in Samain bring together for the first time the theme of innocence and the bucolic setting. Both seem strange and out of place in a book of morbid preoccupations. The theme is obviously the result of a complete emotional swing from the opposite theme of guilt; the setting is a result of previous readings. Their convergence at this point explains the later developments—starting with "Ciles alucinada"—of Herrera's works.

"Ciles alucinada"

In his exploration of a rural world, the expression of monotonous tranquillity was the first step in Herrera's poetic revelation. Thereafter, the disruptions produced by the discovery of human crime shattered this world of primitive calm. In his progress toward a reconciliation, the poet slowly learned to accept the human imperfections which had entered into the world of his imagination.

"Ciles alucinada" is the first poem in which the poet expresses this response. His mask is the young shepherdess Ciles, whose story of love and jealousy constitutes the narrative thread of the poem. Descriptions of the shepherdess in contrasting views of the present and the past give the poem its first movement:

> Ciles es rubia y hermosa. Su niñez como
>   una llama
> se alargó, y a los diez años hubo que hacerle
>   una cama.
> La historia de sus primores hizo en los
>   valles estruendo.
> En su mejilla parece que hay un beso
>   amaneciendo;
> y cuando Ciles suspira lleva el soplo
>   de su boca
> heliotropos insinuantes y ternuras de
>   mandioca.
> Pero Ciles no es la misma desde algún
>   tiempo a esta parte;
> ni siquiera con el cura que va a su casa
>   departe;
> ya los sábados no corre, trémula de regocijo,
> a esperar en el sendero la borrica del
>   cortijo. (p. 117)

The smooth flow of the sixteen-syllable couplets is interrupted only once with an *enjambement* after the first line and an abrupt completion of the sentence: "Su niñez como una llama / se alargó," in which the hyperbaton and the sudden pause reproduce the tense expectation and the surprise the meaning conveys. The last lines quoted are the beginning of a long passage on a theme probably derived from Garcilaso's famous *canción quinta*, "A la flor del Gnido." Ciles is no longer able to enjoy the innocent pleasures that were once her delight, just as the unfortunate lover in Garcilaso's poem shuns the pleasures he formerly sought.

The feelings of the character are projected into the surrounding landscape, which changes in accord with the variable personality of Ciles: misanthropic in her present state of mind, ingenuous when she returns to her former self:

> lloran sus misantropías algunos sauces
>   humanos.
> La hora es cordial. Hasta el ancho azul
>   ingenuo del cielo
> sube el grito del torrente. (p. 118)

An epigraph from Virgil's first eclogue

> Mirabar, quid maesta deos, Amarylli,
>   vocares,
> . . . .
> . . . . ipsae te, Tityre, pinus,
> ipsi te fontes, ipsa haec arbusta vocabant

directs the poet in his vision of nature in sympathy with the plight of the shepherdess. Nature accompanies the girl's changes in mood. When she finally recovers her normal relation to her surroundings, the willow trees become "los sauces fraternales."

Her search for the faithless shepherd Elías is the central event in her life, the adventure that marks her passage from girlhood to maturity, and she undertakes the painful journey with a sense of exhilaration:

> Entre sus labios le tiembla la rosa de
> la aventura. (p. 121)

She walks at night among the inhabitants of an animated and humanized countryside, momentarily invaded by messengers from another world:

> y ella, sin volverse, acaso mira cómo
> de su saya,
> en procesión flavescente que se oculta
> en los barrancos,
> cuelgan su madre que ha muerto y un
> ejército florido
> de ángeles blancos . . . (p. 121)

Her single obsession is to find Elías in order to take revenge on him and then kill herself. But an ecstatic reverie, in Samainian garb, saves young Ciles from her impulsive decision. Here Herrera again uses a traditional theme from Garcilaso's "Egloga segunda," where Albanio is saved from despair by a strange experience. Another model for Herrera y Reissig's poem was possibly the "Prosa ottava" of Sannazaro's *Arcadia*, in which Carino relates how his unhappiness has deeply changed him and how, after an excursion similar to the wanderings of Ciles, when he was about to commit suicide, the appearance of "duo bianchi colombi"[4] made him reconsider. In the same way, Albanio relates that a sudden wind made him fall and lie senseless until,

> con más sano discurso en mi sentido
> comencé de culpar el presupuesto
> y temerario error que había seguido,
>
> en querer dar con triste muerte al resto
> de aquesta breve vida fin amargo,
> no siendo por los hados aún dispuesto.
> (lines 662-667)

Besides repeating traditional bucolic themes, "Ciles alucinada" is reminiscent of the *modernistas* and of the French poets Herrera had recently read. Yet, in spite of the numerous literary associations, this poem marks the beginning of Herrera's acquisition of a personal style. The projection of his emotions into imaginary characters in a simple, rural environment prompted him to describe the commonplace objects of the daily routine. The homely words to which he resorted—"cama," "mandioca," "pasteles," "tocino," "ungüento," "queso," "comedirse," "picar"—are in contrast with the precious vocabulary of some of his earlier poems. In his later writings, the clash of opposite forces finds expression through this conflict in vocabulary, while the diffuse and vague story and the long poem are replaced by precise, instantaneous pictures in the strict pattern of the sonnet, and the familiar attitude of the narrator gives way to a more detailed contemplation of a vivid though momentary creation.

CHAPTER V

A PRIVATE DICTION

After his youthful efforts, Herrera y Reissig discovered the value of the incantatory in reproducing the moods which earlier he had merely described. He felt that he needed to create a system in which the elementary reality of man and nature would mirror itself in symbols, if he was to encompass its variety and apprehend its unity. The multiplicity of appearances was first conquered in momentary visions, but the underlying unity was only dimly apprehended later, when the poet brought together all the intuitions of his private mythology and attempted to build a structure conformable to the communal myths.

The apparent disorder of Herrera's interpretation of reality stems from the simultaneous presence of opposing forces: pleasure and pain, innocence and guilt. The full swing of his imagination from one extreme to the other is paralleled by a quality not yet pointed out by critics, namely, the conflicting nature of his vocabulary, at times homely, almost plebeian, and, in the same poem, luxurious, or remote and dreamlike. This unbalanced vocabulary creates a landscape "seared with trade," or suddenly luminous, but always sharply defined. His word is both apt and unexpected. His line, even when contorted, manages to preserve the rhythm of colloquial speech. Familiar words ("morrongo," "elenco") and prosaic connotations ("digestiones," "improperios," "folletín," "plebeyo") contrast with terms of philosophical import ("Dinamismo Eterno,") or those associated with ideal beauty ("Bethlem," "angélico," "paz"). Moments of ethereal beauty are interrupted by scenes of uncouth human behavior:

>   Hacia la era, inválidos bajo una gloria de oro,
>   vacilan los vehículos en su viaje sonoro . . .
>   Cien rapazuelos llueven ágiles sus guijarros,
>
>   en medio de estridentes júbilos de ludibrio,
>   y, al fin, restableciendo todos el equilibrio,
>   fáciles sabandijas, cuélganse de los carros.
>   (p. 187)

Some lines seem to be bursting with significance because of the diversity of the realms to which the words belong; for such an effect the synaesthetic image is often used:

>   Densos y doctorales, jactan en sus querellas
>   de agrios positivismos. (p. 193)
>   como el·ancho caudillo, que en honor de
>   Pelayo
>   cabalgara montañas, fabuloso y arisco. (p. 194)

> su clara risa entre sus labios rojos
> triscaba como un chorro de agua viva. (p. 239)

Within the perspective of his sonnet, familiar objects are distorted and multiplied in "abismáticos espejos" (p. 240). The commonplace is transfigured in the poet's alchemy by the discovery of secret associations. However, the irreducible core of the grotesque and the ugly can be redeemed only by a kind of negative inclusion: domestic animals and household chores yield to the soft touch of humor, but moral baseness and human frustrations can be conquered only through irony, which forces helpless man to comply with the laws of the infinite, in an ideal foreshortening.

His heterogeneous vocabulary, his playful wit, and his biting irony are all the result of an artistic will to force the different orders of reality into one picture. Every realm of being is called upon to illuminate the meaning of the others:

> Y palomas violetas salen como recuerdos
> de las viejas paredes arrugadas y oscuras.
> (p. 153)

These lines exemplify the kind of figure which interprets natural occurrences by means of psychological phenomena. According to Jorge Luis Borges,[1] these lines of the Uruguayan poet are the most beautiful instance of this figure in the Spanish language.

Herrera's inner struggle is revealed not only in the choice of words but also in the jagged quality of the line: Alexandrines of uneven accents and hendecasyllables of unbalanced rhythms are frequent in his sonnets. Almost entirely absent is the serene iambic hendecasyllable; the Alexandrine shifts the accents of its hemistichs to produce sudden accelerations and unexpected pauses. The details of his style reveal the impressionable temperament of a poet recording momentary sensations. An original belief in universal harmony is tested in his poetry through a sensitiveness to the many sharp edges of the real. This conflict between a belief in harmony and the experience of dissonance was long characteristic of Herrera. Near the end of his short life, the reaffirmation of a moral victory and the conquest of multiplicity slowly emerge, lending to a few of his lines a majesty of sonorous achievement:

y sumo pájaro de las lingüísticas. (p. 270)

In this hendecasyllable, of the *mínimo* variety, the accent on the fourth syllable marks an early peak which, unlike the accents in the more usual types, is not balanced in the next syllables, resulting in the triumphal isolation of the last *esdrújulo*.

The thread that unifies Herrera's collections of poetry follows the vicissitudes of his inner conflict. The qualities of his style—the choice of words, the nervousness of the line, the manifold suggestions—supply the critic with a key to an understanding of his work and permit him to recover its fundamental unity, which has been overlooked because of failure to consider all its diverse aspects.

Los éxtasis de la montaña

Each of the many scenes of *Los éxtasis de la montaña* is a microcosm that reproduces the world seen by the author at a definite moment and in a particular mood. The rural landscape and the village characters are embodiments of the poet's moral knowledge, which became progressively disillusioned. His personal attitude and development found expression in a variety of images and themes that defined and limited his poetic world.

The sonnet "El despertar" opens *Los éxtasis de la montaña* with a mythical vision of the ingenuousness of nature in a mountain village. For a Uruguayan writer, in a country without mountains, this village, at times vaguely located in the Northern Hemisphere, was a product of literary exoticism. The scene of "La misa cándida" is the only one among the sixty Alexandrine sonnets that is obviously laid in the Basque country; it seems an anticipation of the *Sonetos vascos* rather than an integral part of the two series. In his "exotismo europeizante," Herrera placed these bits of imaginary Europe in a pastoral setting, just as many elements of his own immediate environment crept into the distant lands of his exotic writings.

The *eglogánimas*—the subtitle of the two collections—interpret the soul of the ideal countryside they create. The first seven poems depict moods of rural peace and domestic happiness: "El despertar," "El regreso," "El almuerzo," "La siesta," "La velada," "El alba," and "La vuelta de los campos." "La velada," the picture of a simple family group, is a good example:

> La cena ha terminado: legumbres, pan moreno
> y uvas aún lujosas de virginal rocío . . .
> Rezaron ya. La luna nieva un candor sereno
> y el lago se recoge con lácteo escalofrío.
>
> El anciano ha concluido un episodio ameno
> y el grupo desanúdase con un placer cabrío . . .
> Entretanto, allá fuera, en un silencio bueno,
> los campos demacrados encanecen de frío.
>
> Lux canta. Lidé corre. Palemón anda en zancos.
> Todos ríen . . . La abuela demándales sosiego.

> Anfión, el perro, inclina, junto al anciano
>   ciego,
>
> ojos de lazarillo, familiares y francos . . .
> Y al són de las castañas que saltan en
>   el fuego
> palpitan al unísono sus corazones blancos.

The last sonnet of the second series presents a contrasting vision of the same occasion:

> LA CENA
>
> En repique de lata la merienda circula . . .
> Aploma el artesano su crasura y secuestra
> media mesa en canónicas dignidades de bula,
> comiendo con la zurda, por aliviar la
>   diestra . . .
>
> Mientras la grey famélica los manjares
>   adula,
> en sabroso anticipo, sus colmillos adiestra;
> y por merecimiento, casi más que por gula,
> duplica su pitanza de col y de menestra . . .
>
> Luego que ante el rescoldo sus digestiones
>   hipa,
> sumido en la enrulada neblina de su pipa,
> arrullan, golondrinas domésticas de invierno:
>
> la Hormiga, y Blanca Nieves, Caperuza y el
>   Lobo . . .
> Y la prole apollada, bajo el manto materno,
> choca de escalofríos, en un éxtasis bobo.

Adjectives and nouns from different realms—human, natural, and celestial—are repeatedly combined, until the central meaning of the vision emerges: in their innocence, the hearts of these people beat the measure of the natural world, without dissonance.

The juxtaposition of homely and remote or conventionally poetic vocabulary ("legumbres," "pan moreno," "escalofrío," "ameno," "cabrío," "zancos," "castañas"—"luna," "candor," "lago,") correlates the different worlds in an essential unity. The last lines summarize symbolically all the suggestions summoned up by the interaction of words and images. Two sensations, the cracking of roasted chestnuts and the beating of human hearts, polarize the multiple meanings that arise from the succession of images. It is only when the sonnet is completed that the first line,

> La cena ha terminado: legumbres, pan moreno,

a bare statement of fact, is illuminated. With the final symbols, the intervening images become integrated and react on this initial sentence.

In "La cena" the juxtaposition in vocabulary does not bring together the homely and the remote, but the ugly and the pretentious. The excessive dignity of such words as "canónicas," "dignidades," "famélica," "adula" is ironically contrasted with the moral, intellectual, and physical inferiority of the group and the unrefined vocabulary: "lata," "crasura," "zurda," "colmillos," "hipa." This contrast becomes even more violent when the term "bobo" follows "éxtasis," preceded by the indirect presentation of the mother's personality in a humorous image. Dissonant sensations of unpleasant vividness—"un repique de lata," "sus digestiones hipa"—replace the joyful sounds and the "good silence" of "La velada." The major themes of *Los éxtasis de la montaña* become clear in a comparison of the first lines of the two poems:

> La cena ha terminado: legumbres, pan moreno
> En repique de lata la merienda circula.

When illuminated by the succeeding elements in the poem, the first line is emblematical of rural life in its beauty and innocence. The second line, associated with the commonplace vulgarity of a rustic dinner, represents the poet's discovery of the unlovely.

Between these extremes, Herrera draws some sympathetic and some ironic portraits of village characters. In the first series he could portray human vanity with tolerance:

> Arrodíllase, y sobre su contrita insolencia
> guiña la eterna y muda comba interrogadora.
> (p. 172)

But in a later poem his caricature of a physician admits no redeeming qualities:

> Flamante con sus gafas sin muchos retintines
> ataca a sus enfermos el médico cazurro:
> al bien forrado, es lógico, lo cura con latines
> y en cuanto al pobre, rápido receta desde el
> burro. (p. 180)

In the early poems the village folk are playfully united in an atmosphere of contentment. The barber, "folletín de la aldea," the humble and pious priest, the loving swains, live in an Arcadia where sin and crime are unknown. But toward the end of the first collection, and sporadically in the second series, the peasant becomes immoderately concerned with material needs, and his moral nature is defined in a daring synaesthesia:

> Y mientras el probable rendimiento calcula,
> con un pan de la víspera entretiene su
>   gula . . .
> Sabe un gusto a consorte en la masa harto
>   linda. (p. 169)

Youthful lovers are no longer innocent, as in the early sonnets, and their joy turns into melancholy self-torture as they discover guilt. In an early poem, Edipo and Diana experience an uncontaminated pleasure, suggested in an ethereal image:

> ¡y así las horas pasan en su inocente riña,
> como una suave pluma por unos bellos
>   labios! (p. 159)

The lovers of a later poem discover "... la incitante fruta de ajena cerca,"¹ and the shepherdess expresses in her gestures the need for modesty:

> Y ella en púdicas grimas, con dignidades
>   tiernas
> de doncellez, se frunce el percal que recata
> la primicia insinuante de sus prósperas
>   piernas ... (p. 167)

In "Extasis" the lovers evoke "perdidas inocencias." In "El espejo" there is conflict and self-torture: "Por no verla, en procura de un instante de calma."

The concern with sexual guilt appears only sporadically in *Los éxtasis de la montaña*, but becomes central in the later collection, *Los parques abandonados*. Nevertheless, it is part of Herrera's disillusionment with the rural community he had created, and it enters into the pictures of the monotonous dog days, as in "Canícula," one of the last poems:

> zagales y zagalas se unen sobre la hierba ...

Many of the sonnets, mostly in the second series, deal directly with the monotony of village life. The contentment of the villagers gives way to frustration and boredom. "Domingo" in the first series and "Dominus vobiscum" in the second series deal with the same subject. An idyllic vision is presented in the

playful lines of the first sonnet, in which the Sabbath
is interpreted in a euphoric image:

> ¡Oh domingo! La infancia de espíritu te
>   sueña
> y el pobre mendicante que es el que más
>   te ordeña . . .

In "Dominus vobiscum," Sunday is just a drone among the days of the week. Although the sky is still blessing the village, the tourists and their automobiles disturb the peace and beauty of the landscape:

> Bosteza el buen domingo, zángano de
>   semana . . .
> El trapero del burgo ronda las callejuelas;
> y enluta el Seminario, en dos sordas estelas,
> su desfile simétrico, de una misma sotana.
>
> Junto a la fuente, donde chocan las
>   castañuelas
> los sapos, el "elenco" debuta en la tartana;
> y beato, sobre tantas mansedumbres abuelas
> el cielo inclina un gesto de bendición
>   cristiana.
>
> Dos turistas, muñecos rubios de rostro
>   inmóvil,
> maniobran la visita de un fogoso automóvil . . .
> Con su lente y sus frascos y su equipo de
>   viaje,
>
> investiga el zootécnico, profesor de
>   lombrices,
> y a su vera, dos chicos, en un gesto salvaje,
> atisban, con los húmedos dedos en las
>   narices.

The words that imply moral value, "buen," "bendición," "beato," "cristiana," are applied to the abstract day and the distant sky; the condemnation of the village is expressed only by the impact of visual images: the toads, the tourists, the zoölogist, and the children, progressively and regrettably more unpleasant. The initial line, with its two balanced and contrasting hemistichs, becomes a double picture of the opposite and complementary villages, living side by side in the higher truth of the poems.

Sonetos vascos

The Spanish American *modernistas* were attracted by the cosmopolitan cities of Europe, and seldom tried to capture the simplicity of country manners. But Herrera chose the colorful background of the Basque country and its picturesque customs as the setting for his *Sonetos vascos*, nine Alexandrine sonnets written in 1906. His knowledge of the Basque setting was vicarious, however, since he never traveled outside the River Plate region. The Uruguayan writer followed the trend prevalent among Spanish writers of the Generation of '98, who depicted the pueblo with loving exactness.

The literary sources of these sonnets are often unrelated to the Basque country itself. The "molinos de aventura" are evidently of Cervantine origin; equally incongruous are literary allusions to Hernani, Don Quijote, Sancho, Tartarin, and Cyrano. From the Carlista wars of the nineteenth-century, however, Herrera derived the guerrilla leader and priest, a genuine Basque type. The Cura Santa Cruz, in Unamuno's episodic novel *Paz en la guerra* (1897), and José Fago, in Benito Pérez Galdós' *Zumalacárregui* (1898), may have been the inspiration for Herrera's "curas con fusiles." Galdós' novel supplied him with a study of an inner conflict that must have been his model for the best poem of the series, "El jefe negro."

From Spanish writers of the early twentieth century—Unamuno, Azorín, Valle Inclán—came also his interest in the history of Spain, its past glory and its present decadence. These new elements in Herrera's poetry are fused with his central search for moral knowledge, revealed in the repeated use of the word "bueno." The countryside Herrera recreated in this collection had been the subject of the sonnet "La misa cándida" in *Los éxtasis de la montaña:*

> Jardín de rosa angélico, la tierra guipuzcoana.
> Edén que un Fra Doménico soñara en
>   acuarelas . . .
> Los hombres tienen rostros vírgenes de
>   manzana,
> y son las frescas mozas óleos de antiguas
>   telas.
>
> Fingen en la apretura de la calleja aldeana
> secretearse las casas con chismosas
>   cautelas.
> Y estimula el buen ocio un trin-trin de
>   campanas,
> un pum-pum de timbales y un fron-fron de
>   vihuelas.
>
> ¡Oh campo siempre niño! ¡Oh patria de alma
>   proba!
> Como una virgen, mística de tramonto, se
>   arroba . . .
> Aves, mar, bosques: todo ruge, solloza y
>   trina
>
> las bienaventuranzas sin código y sin
>   reyes . . .
> ¡Y en medio a ese sonámbulo coro de
>   Palestrina,
> oficia la apostólica dignidad de los bueyes!

The Basque country is depicted as an angelic place. There is no conflict, no struggle. Even the "ocio" of its people is "buen ocio." The perfection of the country is stressed in the last lines; it is compared to a child, said to have an honest soul, to be like a virgin—ignorant of sin—and to live in happiness without laws or kings: the real Golden Age. The language of the homely—"calleja aldeana," "secretearse," "chismosas"—is endowed with a playful, childlike grace, until the onomatopoeic "trin-trin," "pum-pum," and "fron-fron" are resorted to for the expression of a euphoric moment.

In the poems of *Sonetos vascos*, the Golden Age of harmony, peace, and goodness has changed to a strident world of offensive colors. In "Vizcaya" the musical instruments are no longer the bells, kettledrums, and guitars of "La misa cándida" but the shriller fifes and tambourines. In the same poem, "curas . . . y bandidos" hint at the duality of Christianity and war and crime. Here the poet finds the root of his rejection of human nature. Yet the characters preserve the virtues of nobility and courage, even in the portrait of "El mayoral," in which Herrera echoed the concern of the Generation of '98 with Spanish decadence and *abulia*, although the Basque region is probably the least appropriate for such a presentation:

> Con la faja incendiaria de crujiente
>   pingajo,
> con su boina arrogante de carlismo y sus
>   prendas,
> ruge el viejo Pelayo sus morriñas tremendas,
> y sus "jes" y sus "erres" desenfunda a
>   destajo . . .
>
> Nadie anima una yunta, nadie blande las
>   riendas,
> como el Cid montonero campeador del atajo;
> juega en su modo el guante dócil del agasajo
> y le ofusca un invierno de lejanas
>   leyendas . . .

> El eco de sus bélicos alaridos rebota
> de valle en monte, en ágiles balances de
>   pelota . . .
> En su regia cabeza y en su garbo de roble,
>
> se recela un instinto algo terco de cabra . . .
> Y soslaya sus ojos de mastín bravo y noble
> el orgullo que roe la tristeza cantabra.

The sonnet expresses both the irony of the grandeur Spain had known, reduced now to the futility of a minor war, and the permanence of ancient courage and glory in the guerrilla fighter: "el Cid montonero campeador del atajo." The glorious associations of the past ("Cid," "campeador") are contrasted with commonplace reality ("montonero," "atajo").

The sonnet "El jefe negro" expresses Herrera's condemnation as well as his final acceptance of human nature through a deeper understanding. Here the intensity of thought has produced a concentrated and forceful poem:

> Temerario y agudo y diestro entre los diestros
> el jefe negro empuña su indómita mesnada;
> y en pos de bendiciones o al són de padre-
>   nuestros,
> desata las guerrillas y asorda la
>   emboscada . . .
>
> Comulgan en su alforja con los bandos
>   siniestros
> el cáliz, y con chumbos la Custodia Sagrada.
> Canta misas en medio de los bosques
>   ancestros,
> y del santo responso pasa a la cuchillada.
>
> Espeluzna en su neutra virilidad de eunuco
> el rosario enroscado a un enorme trabuco . . .
> ¡Oh buen león! Apenas bate el hierro
>   inhumano

> para orar por el alma del vencido se vuelve:
> el enemigo pronto se convierte en hermano
> y la mano que mata es la mano que
> absuelve ... !

The contradiction that runs through the sonnet collection is more painful here because the sacred symbols of Christianity and the instruments and scenes of warfare have been brought together. Image contrasts with image in a rapid succession of conflicting signs in the first nine lines, leading to an impetuous crescendo in the tenth line:

> el rosario enroscado a un enorme trabuco.

This complex symbol—an image endowed with a multiplicity of suggestions—is contrasted immediately with "buen león." Without pausing to explain the logical links, the poet has embodied his thought in two successive symbols, paradoxical in themselves and mutually contradictory. The rosary wound around a musket is the culminating point of the criminal fusion of religion and war. Abruptly, from depths of despair, comes the discovery of a moral superiority in this warrior-priest who absolves the foe he wounded. Goodness and courage ("buen león") redeem him in the midst of cruelty.

When the unlovely and the morally base have been conquered, the characters are presented through unequivocal symbols of courage and honesty. "El caudillo" is the result of this new attitude:

> Ya que baile o que ría, ya que ruja o que
> cante,
> en la lid o en la gresca, nadie atreve un
> desplante,
> nadie erige tan noble rebelión como el vasco,

> y sobre esa leonina majestad que le orla,
> le revienta la boina de valor como un casco
> que tuviera por mecha encendida la borla . . . !

The beret is the image that interprets the nature of the Basque, his nobility and valor. Similarly, in the last poem of the series, "El granjero," the "diamantes de honradez" represent his honesty.

Los parques abandonados

Of the sixty-five sonnets that comprise the two collections, eleven[3] can be approximately dated, since they were published in the magazine *Vida Moderna* of Montevideo in June, 1903. The eleven poems are to be considered part of the early, immature work of Herrera, who, at the time of publication, intended to incorporate them into the book *Los maitines de la noche*. Most of the other sonnets of *Los parques abandonados* were written several years later, probably in 1908. The decision to gather them under the Verlainean title and the subtitle "Eufocordias" was of later date, also. These "harmonies of the heart" are of uneven quality. At times they echo Romantic writers, even paraphrase their poems: the sonnet "El juego" is an adaptation of Heine's "Wir haben viel für einander gefühlt," from *Lyrisches Intermezzo*, known to Herrera in the translation of the Venezuelan poet Juan Antonio Pérez Bonalde, published in 1877. The epigraph of "El juego" translates the last line of Heine's poem, "Dasz wir uns nimmermehr wiederfinden," as "Que nunca llegaremos a encontrarnos . . ."

Jugando al escondite, en dulce aparte,
niños o pájaros los dos, me acuerdo,
por gustar tu inquietud casi me pierdo,
y en cuanto a ti . . . ¡problema era
 encontrarte . . . !

Después, cuando el espíritu fué cuerdo,
burló mi amor tu afán en ocultarte . . .
y al amarme a tu vez, en el recuerdo
de otra mujer me refugié con arte.

De nuevo, en la estación de la experiencia,
diste en buscarme, cuando yo en la ausencia,
suerte fatal, me disfracé de olvido . . .

Por fin, el juego ha terminado . . . ¡Trunca
tu vida fué! . . . Tan bien te has escondido,
que, ¡vive Dios! ¡no nos veremos nunca! . . .

In *Los parques abandonados*, Herrera uses the pastoral décor he had derived from French sources, but the setting is only vaguely sketched and not always rural. Melancholy parks alternate with farmhouses and country scenes. In harmony with the shadowy background, the contrasts in vocabulary are also subdued. Except for a few poems, mostly in the second series, the thoughts and emotions are less vivid than in *Los éxtasis de la montaña*, at times even artificial. In the use of religious terminology when dealing with profane love, in the first book mainly, the author seems only to be following an old convention popular among *modernistas* on both sides of the Atlantic: it is found, among others, in Rubén Darío, in the *Sonatas* of Ramón María del Valle Inclán, and in Enrique Rodríguez Larreta's *La gloria de don Ramiro*.[4] Herrera, because of his more intense and persistent nature, continued longer in the same trend and, after this first decorative use of religious terms, tried, in *Las clepsidras* (1910), to express the essential unity of divine and human love. Evidently, the terminology did not indicate a sincere faith on the part of the author, who still adhered to vague monistic beliefs. In him a Catholic imagination accompanied non-Catholic conceptions. The central poem of the first series of *Los parques abandonados* is "Luna de miel," wherein the experience is interpreted through the imagery of religion.

The clash of reality and illusion is evident in the contrast in vocabulary, which at times attains the intensity of his previous books:

> hallé un sendero matinal de estrellas
> en tu falda ilusión de rosa claro. (p. 199)

The violent juxtaposing of two nouns telescopes the prosaic and the ideal. But in the next sonnets the poet deals with the earthly imperfections of love—infidelity, jealousy, guilt. The changing attitude of the author is revealed by images referring to unpleasant sensations: "roncos tenores," "agrias tonadas," "gesto oscuro." The distant sound of the barking of a dog is endowed with the power to rebound, as the symbol of a disquieting mystery:

> ¡mientras, en los cortijos soñolientos
> rebotaba de pronto algún ladrido! . . . (p. 207)

The last sonnet of the first series, "Color de sueño," synthesizes the poet's initial understanding of human love. After this experience he is visited in dreams by a wounded person whom he does not recognize. The identity of the nightly visitor is revealed only in the last lines:

> quién eres, al fin, la interrogué, me dijo:
> —Ya ni siquiera me conoces, hijo:
> ¡si soy tu alma que ha sufrido tanto! . . .

In a few poems in the second series, Herrera turns from human love to the mystery of existence. Here he uses the same religious terminology ("hostias," "corderos") with reference to a sacrifice at the altar of knowledge:

> ¡Oh tú, de incienso místico la más delgada
>   espira,
> lámpara taciturna y Anfora de soñar!
> Eres toda la Esfinge y eres toda la Lira
> y eres el abismático pentagrama del mar.
>
> ¡Oh Sirena melódica en que el Amor conspira,
> encarnación sonámbula de una aurora lunar!
> Toma de mis corderos blancos para tu pira
> y haz de mis trigos blancos hostias para
>   tu altar.
>
> ¡Oh Catedral hermética de carne visigoda!
> A ti van las heráldicas cigüeñas de mi Oda.
> En ti beben mis labios, vaso de toda Ciencia.
>
> ¡Lírica sensitiva que la muerte restringe!
> ¡Salve, noche estrellada y urna de
>   quintaesencia:
> eres toda la Lira y eres toda la Esfinge!

Many sonnets of the second part of *Los parques abandonados*, however, continue the main thematic threads of the first series. The concern with guilt is the subject of "La culpa," "Oleo brillante," and others. Infidelity is interpreted in "La intrusa":

> ¡Ay! si te viera cuánto te amaría
> la triste soledad, tu rival, esa
> que odias y es apenas una sombra! . . .

The indifference of woman and her heartlessness are themes of poems influenced by Gustavo Adolfo Bécquer, a dependence that is clear in the lines:

¡a qué insistir! si esa mujer no siente,
si no sabe sentir, ¡ni nunca ha amado! (p. 236)

The book ends, nevertheless, with poems in which the author reaffirms his belief in the unity of the universe and the correspondence of human and divine love. The ecstatic compenetration with the All, the "consubstanciación" of Herrera's vocabulary, is the subject of the sonnet "Panteísmo":

> Los dos sentimos ímpetus reflejos,
> oyendo, junto al mar, los fugitivos
> sueños de Gluck, y por los tiempos viejos
> rodaron en su tez oros furtivos . . .
>
> La luna hipnotizaba nimbos vivos,
> surgiendo entre abismáticos espejos,
> Calló la orquesta, y descendió a lo lejos
> un enigma de puntos suspensivos . . .
>
> Luego: la inmensidad, el astro, el hondo
> silencio, todo penetró hasta el fondo
> de nuestro ser . . . Un inaudito halago
>
> de consubstanciación y aéreo giro
> electrizónos, y hacia el éter vago
> subimos en la gloria de un suspiro . . .

In the five series of sonnets, defining the clarity of each object which he paused to interpret mythically, the poet has expressed in his private diction his mental reactions to the conflicting and puzzling multiplicity of appearances. From a sentimental acceptance of a total unity, and then the discovery of ugliness and moral wrong, he has proceeded at last to a serene inclusion of the diverse elements of nature and to a reconciliation with life's imperfections. After projecting his momentary visions into contradictory scenes and symbols, Herrera needed now to synthesize and order his thematic interests and fragmentary intuitions within a structure of larger scope.

CHAPTER VI

EXPERIMENTS IN

STRUCTURE

The *Sonetos vascos* and *Los parques abandonados* form a bridge in the poet's passage from the private mythology of *Los éxtasis de la montaña* to the literary myths of his last works. The semihistorical subject matter of *Sonetos vascos* and the conventional religious terminology of *Los parques abandonados* prepare the poet for a return to the myths of the community. "La muerte del pastor" (1907) belongs to approximately this same stage in Herrera's development.

"La muerte del pastor" is written in the traditional eight-syllable line, interrupted at times by a four-syllable line and by groups of three four-syllable feet. The poem is unique among Herrera's works for simplicity and serene beauty. Built around a symbolic "carreta" that appears several times, it is a moving elegy on the death of a shepherd. The fidelity of his beloved is the quality that redeems feminine love and reconciles the poet to its imperfections. Again he can see the shepherdess as an innocent being and reverts to one of his favorite comparisons:

> Su corazón va llorando
> como un cordero inexperto.

The shepherdess' increasing awareness of the irrevocable nature of her loss is paralleled in the crescendo of the poem. At first it seems to her that he is only delayed:

> ¡Cuánto tarda la carreta!

But the delay is prolonged:

> Hoy se tarda más que nunca la carreta.

Then there is the realization that he will not return:

> Ya no verás la carreta
> por el atajo vecino
>
> Hoy no viene la carreta.

The full significance of death is finally stated through the same symbol:

> Nunca vendrá la carreta.

The oxcart becomes a mythical presence in the rural community Herrera has created. He endows it with the reality of a legendary life on a second imaginary level:

> Mas ciertas noches, no hay duda,
> cuenta la grey rusticana,
> suele verse una carreta
> y detrás una serrana
> tocando la pandereta,
> por el camino violeta
> que conduce a la fontana . . .

Toward the end of his life, Herrera sought to organize larger and more complex poetic structures. The mythical interpretation of fragments of time, in their diversity, no longer sufficed. Instead of continuing the trend initiated with "La muerte del pastor," he wrote a series of sonnets, *Las clepsidras* (1910), more closely unified than most of the earlier ones. He wished to bring together the myths of different religions and the exotic décor of different lands in order to express his belief in a central unity.

The attempt to integrate diverse myths had been prefigured in the early poem, *Las Pascuas del Tiempo*, and was a central interest in "La torre de las esfinges" (1909), a long cryptic poem on the problem of good and evil. These two poems express the rebellion and blasphemous attitude of Herrera, as an heir of the Decadents. He later transcends them in the deeper understanding of *Las clepsidras*, which contains some of his most successful poems.

"La torre de las esfinges" and "Berceuse blanca"

In the tortured poetry of "La torre de las esfinges," the poet again faces moral problems. Just as the "carreta" was the unifying symbol of "La muerte del pastor" and time the unifying element in *Las Pascuas del Tiempo*, in "La torre de las esfinges" Herrera seems to have intended to build the poem around the figure of King Oedipus. Such a possibility may be inferred from the Greek epigraph that accompanies the poem:

> Ah me! ah woe is me!
> Ah whither am I borne!
> How like a ghost forlorn
> My voice flits from me on the air!
> (Translated by F. Storr)

These words are uttered by Oedipus when he appears on stage just after he has discovered the monstrous depth of his guilt and has blinded himself. If these words were intended to focus the central theme, "La torre de las esfinges" must have been meant to express human rebelliousness against the fate that has deluded the innocent hero into the greatest of crimes. This theory may be strengthened by a fragmentary preoccupation with universal evil, symbolized in the Biblical Leviathan and associated with Baudelairean ennui:

> En un bostezo de horror
> tuerce el estero holgazán
> su boca de Leviatán
> tornasolada de horror ...

Unfortunately, "La torre de las esfinges" is intelligible only in part. The grotesqueness of the images and the excess of literary, legendary, and artistic allusions—a continuation of the poetry "de cultura"—contribute to the hermeticism of the poem, which here seems to be the result of a vain attempt to explore the tragic essence of guilt. The poet calls to mind not only the symbolical Leviathan and the incestuous crime of the unfortunate king, but also the myth of the Fall in his desire to encompass the totality of evil:

> En el Edén de la inquieta
> ciencia del Bien y del Mal,
> mordí en tu beso el fatal
> manzano de carne inquieta.

The *décimas* of "La torre de las esfinges" have made uncomfortable reading for most critics because of their decadent and morbid references and their pretentious vocabulary: "cataléptico," "pitagorizador," "horoscopa," "auto-reproche," "espectroscopio," "hicocervos," "metempsicosis," "aneurisma," "hiperestesia," "electrosis," "uremia," "escolopendra."

"Berceuse blanca" has won acclaim, however; it expresses rebellion against fate, but without the strange vocabulary:

> ¡Duerme! Cuando durmamos la eterna y la
> macabra,
> la insensible y la única embriaguez que no
> alegra,
> y sea tu himeneo la Esfinge sin palabra,
> y el ataúd el tálamo de nuestra boda negra,
>
> con llantos y suspiros mi alma entre la fosa
> dará calor y vida para tu carne yerta,
> y con sus dedos frágiles de marfil y de rosa
> desflorará tus ojos sonámbulos de muerta! . . .

The idea in these lines, of course, echoes Baudelaire's "Une Charogne," and is the climax of a long series of Alexandrine quatrains. The setting is the beloved's chamber and the scene is derived from the third canto of Musset's "Rolla":

> ¡Oh levedad de líneas! ¡Oh esbeltez de
> contorno! . . .
> Algo rueda, algo late en la oscura armonía . . .
> Es tan bella que el Angel azul que vela en
> torno
> se interroga temblando si es su amante o su
> guía.

A stanza inspired in Musset's:

> Le petit chérubin qui veille sur son âme
> Doute s'il est son frère ou s'il est son
> amant.[1]

Not only are the central idea and the setting derivative, but the rhythm itself, and some images and even lines are obviously modeled after Darío's "Sonatina":

> ¡Cómo sueña la Virgen! ¿Soñará en cosas
> vanas,
> en su hermana la rosa desmayada en un vaso,
> en el mago Aladino o en las otras hermanas
> que hartarán de bombones su zapato de raso?

> está mudo el teclado de su clave sonoro;
> y en un vaso olvidada se desmaya una flor.[1]
> ....
> ¿Piensa acaso en el príncipe de Golconda o
>   de China,
> o en el que ha detenido su carroza argentina
> para ver de sus ojos la dulzura de luz?

Even more indicative of the decline of Herrera's faculties—"Berceuse blanca" was written during his last days—are the numerous repetitions of images and lines from his own earlier poems, mostly from the second part of *Los parques abandonados*:

> ¡Eres toda la Lira y eres toda la Esfinge!
>
> Sauce abstraído y arpa muda, vaso de Ciencia
>
> noche estrellada y urna blanca de
>   quintaesencia

repeat, almost to the word, lines from the sonnet "Eres todo..." The lines:

> ¡Cuantas veces mi alma pendió, muda a su
>   lado,
> de la dilatación perla de una sonrisa!

are almost identical with lines from "El drama del silencio," also from the second part of *Los parques abandonados*:

> Mi alma pendía como una violeta
> de la dilatación de tu sonrisa.

The Oriental and the pastoral settings usual in Herrera appear in a stanza which describes a piece of tapestry and provides a running commentary to the main theme: the assertion of the poet's faithfulness, which is repeated, with slight variations, six times:

> ¡Silencio, oh luz, silencio! ¡Pliega tu faz,
>   mi Lirio!
> No has menester de Venus filtros para
>   vencerme.
> Mi pensamiento vela como un dragón asirio.
> Duerme, no temas nada. ¡Duerme, mi vida,
>   duerme! . . .

The counterpart to this main theme, the Oriental shepherdess wounded by Cupid, appears twice:

> —En el tapiz de Oriente, a la sombra de un
>   dátil,
> una pastora sueña con el alma inclinada,
> sin mirar que a su vera, desde amable
>   emboscada,
> le insinúa una flecha el arquero versátil.

The main theme, the subordinate theme of the Oriental shepherdess, and the stanzas describing the peace and beauty of the moment form an intricate pattern, which, after several repetitions, comes to a climax in the central idea of the poem, in the last two stanzas.

Las clepsidras

The nineteen sonnets of this collection—the last major poetic effort of Herrera y Reissig—are subtitled "Cromos exóticos" because they deal with myths of different religions and their décor is suggestive of distant worlds. Since these sonnets are chromolithographs depicting the brilliant colors of foreign lands, they may be related to those of the Parnassians. Nevertheless, they are not intended to be accurate descriptions; myths and varied settings are freely combined for the sole purpose of expressing the poet's emotions.

Toward the end of his life, Herrera's interest in Oriental and Biblical myths had become almost obsessive, and he gave free rein to his enthusiasm: "¡Oh, el Oriente; niño inmortal con grandes barbas de color y cuernos de inspirado! ¡Oh, el Oriente de las pesadillas; oh, el Oriente puro, místico y grave; oh, el niño miedoso, oh, el niño poeta!"[3] But the pagan Orient is joined with Greek and Christian myths in *Las clepsidras*. Herrera was trying to encompass the geographical world of this earth and the historical world of the mind. India was called upon to supply mystery and the religious attitude of reverence and worship; Greece, the light of pure reason. The Middle Ages appear as a symbol of naïveté. Africa contributes its primitive and savage cruelty; Arabia, a languid, melancholy sensuality.

Herrera is most successful in the two central sonnets of the series, "Fecundidad" and "Génesis," which present the myth of creation in two equivalent forms, Christian and pagan, which agree that life mirrors divine existence and is a product of divine love. In the first sonnet, on the myth of the Fall, the main idea is symbolized in the image "iris," with its meanings of rainbow, the human eye, and the flower—an ambiguity that indicates the correspondence of the three realms, celestial, human, and natural:

> "¡Adán, Adán, un beso!", dijo, y era
> que en una gemebunda sacudida
> el absurdo nervioso de la vida
> le hizo temblar el dorso y la cadera.
>
> El iris floreció como una ojera
> exótica. Y el "¡ay!" de una caída
> fué el más dulce dolor. Y fué una herida.
> La más roja y eterna primavera.

"¡Adán, Adán, procúrame un veneno!"
dijo, y en una crispación flagrante
la eternidad atravesóle el seno...

Entonces comenzó a latir el mundo.
Y el sol colgaba del cenit, triunfante
como un ígneo testículo fecundo.

"Génesis," supposedly a Greek version of the same mythical wisdom, expounds the correspondence of the divinity and the world in a narrative of the creation of the Milky Way as a result of a rapture of the child Hercules:

Los astros tienen las mejillas tiernas...
La luna trunca es una paradoja
espectro-humana. Proserpina arroja
su sangre al mar. Las horas son eternas.

Júpiter en la orgía desenoja
su ceño absurdo; y junto a las cisternas,
las Ménades, al sol que las sonroja,
arman la columnata de sus piernas.

Juno duerme cien noches... Vorazmente,
Hércules niño, con precoz desvelo,
en un lúbrico rapto de serpiente,

le muerde el seno. Brama el Helesponto...
Surge un lampo de leche. Y en el cielo
la Vía Láctea escintiló de pronto.

The indifference of feminine laughter, a theme derived from Darío, becomes now the definition of woman's essence and her necessary function:

Ríes y evoca tu reír festivo

los grillos de oro del Amor cautivo;
y juraría que tu beso sella
eternidades con el lacre vivo. (p. 269)

The final reconciliation with the guilt and evil symbolized in the feminine "tú" of "La torre de las esfinges" produced a revaluation of the experience of love. Several poems of the series are devoted to a definition of woman and the relationship of human love to the attainment of divine knowledge. The sonnet "Reina del arpa y del amor" is an example:

> ¡Vamos a Dios! Entre floridos cánticos,
> piquen tus dedos, pájaros románticos,
> el Arpa antigua del vergel de Sión . . .
>
> Y alzando a ti mi beso, en un hipnótico
> rapto de azul, como en un cáliz gótico
> beberé el vino de tu corazón.

Considered as isolated units, the sonnets of *Las clepsidras* are only further examples of the poet's keen vision of the momentary in fragments of original imagery. Nevertheless, his attempt to unify them through traditional myths indicates that he had turned from the values of personal expression to those of general communication. Transcending the disconnected pictures of Symbolist and Impressionist technique, Herrera attempted, in his last works, to incorporate the manifold facets of his thought in the completeness of a larger structure.

Present in his later poetry, and at times presaged in earlier works, are the rudiments of an effort at synthesis. The telescoping of myths in search of the universal behind the common experiences of the race, and the moral concerns of his poetry testify to Herrera's conscious quest for an all-inclusive pattern into which to project his imaginative life. But in spite of the exquisite artistry of "La muerte del pastor" and a few sonnets in *Las clepsidras*, the major works of his last years fail in their ambitious attempt to synthesize the themes and mythology of the modern world in a complex whole. And yet this self-contradictory desire for totality and the obsession with the momentary go far to explain his work and his personality. The numerous fragments of crystalline or of tortured poetry which he left place Herrera y Reissig as one of the most successful of the immediate disciples of Rubén Darío in Spanish America. Both by the daring quality of his images and his attempts to transcend the boundaries of the purely personal, Herrera pointed the way for the poets who wrote after the days of the *modernista* movement in the River Plate region.

NOTES

NOTES TO CHAPTER I

[1] Jorge Guillén, *La poética de Bécquer*, p. 18.
[2] Julián del Casal, *Poesías completas*, pp. 135, 239.
[3] Enrique Díez Canedo, *Letras de América*, p. 396.
[4] Manuel Gutiérrez Nájera, "El cruzamiento en literatura," *Revista Azul*, September 9, 1894, pp. 289-292.
[5] On this point see Arturo Torres-Rioseco, "Las teorías poéticas de Poe y el caso de José Asunción Silva," *Hispanic Review*, XVIII (1950), 319-327.
[6] José Asunción Silva, *Prosas y versos*, pp. 110, 154.
[7] Rubén Darío, *Obras completas*, XVII, 171.
[8] ". . . a la sazón la lucha simbolista apenas comenzaba en Francia y no era conocida en el Extranjero, y menos en nuestra América," *ibid.*, p. 170.
[9] Francisco Rodríguez Marín, ed., *Obras de Pedro de Espinosa*.
[10] On this point see Juan López Morillas, "El *Azul* de Rubén Darío. ¿Galicismo mental o lingüístico?" *Revista Hispánica Moderna*, X (1944), 9-14.
[11] Rubén Darío, "Los colores del estandarte," *La Nación*, November 27, 1896, in *Escritos inéditos de Rubén Darío*, p. 121.
[12] *Los raros* included articles on E. A. Poe, Leconte de Lisle, Paul Verlaine, Villiers de l'Isle Adam, Léon Bloy, Jean Richepin, Jean Moréas, Rachilde, George d'Esparbès, Augusto de Armas, Laurent Tailhade, Fra Domenico Cavalca, Eduardo Dubus, Theodore Hannon, Lautréamont, Max Nordau, Ibsen, José Martí, and Eugenio de Castro. In the 1901 edition the sketch "El arte en silencio," on Camille Mauclair, and a sketch on Paul Adam were added.
[13] Jules Huret, *Enquête sur l'évolution littéraire*, p. 67. Previously published in *L'Echo de Paris*, 1891.

¹⁴Darío, op. cit., pp. 123, 134-137.
¹⁵Rafael Cansinos-Asséns, "Un interesante poema de S. M.," *Cervantes* (Madrid, 1919). See also Alfonso Reyes, "Mallarmé en espagnol," *Revue de Littérature Comparée*, XII (1932), 546-568.
¹⁶Juan Ramón Jiménez, "Crisis del espíritu en la poesía española contemporánea," *Nosotros*, XII (1940), 167.
¹⁷Federico de Onís y Sánchez, *Antología de la poesía española e hispanoamericana* (1882-1932), p. 470.
¹⁸Alberto Zum Felde, *Proceso intelectual del Uruguay* . . . , p. 211.
¹⁹Herminia Herrera y Reissig, *Vida íntima de Julio Herrera y Reissig*, p. 65.
²⁰For a study of the "Generación del 900," see Emir Rodríguez Monegal, *José E. Rodó en el novecientos*, pp. 15-39; for a detailed discussion of the relations between Herrera y Reissig and Rodó, see the chapter "Algunos coetáneos," pp. 83-92.

NOTES TO CHAPTER II

¹Paul Valéry, "Situation de Baudelaire," *Variété II*, p. 174.
²Alberto Zum Felde, *Proceso intelectual del Uruguay* . . . , p. 268.
³Mora Magela Flores, *Julio Herrera y Reissig* . . . , p. 30.
⁴Herrera y Reissig, *Obras completas*, V, 71. Hereafter abbreviated *Obras*.
⁵*La Revista*, November 5, 1899, pp. 169-170.
⁶Herrera y Reissig, *Poesías completas*, p. 107. Page references are hereafter given in the text.
⁷Rubén Darío, *Prosas profanas*, p. 16.
⁸*Obras*, V, 113.
⁹Elizabeth Colquhoun, "Notes on French Influences in the Work of Julio Herrera y Reissig," *Bulletin of Spanish Studies*, XXI (1944), 158.
¹⁰Stéphane Mallarmé, *Œuvres complètes*, p. 241.
¹¹*Obras*, III, 12. See Colquhoun, op. cit., p. 155.
¹²*Obras*, III, 21-22.
¹³*Ibid.*, III, 14.
¹⁴Colquhoun, op. cit., p. 153.
¹⁵Svend Johansen, *Le Symbolisme*, p. 21.
¹⁶On this point see the unanimous testimony of several

critics and personal friends of the poets, in *Nosotros*, May-June, 1938.

¹⁷T. S. Eliot, "The Possibility of a Poetic Drama," *The Sacred Wood*, p. 63.

¹⁸For a detailed analysis of these reminiscences see Colquhoun, *op. cit.*, pp. 146-153.

¹⁹On the other hand, Elizabeth Colquhoun, *op. cit.*, p. 150, sees a similarity between "Xanthis" and "La flauta," of the first series of *Los éxtasis de la montaña*.

NOTES TO CHAPTER III

¹Charles Baudelaire, "Eureka," *Œuvres complètes*, VII, 471.

²Albert Thibaudet, *La Poèsie de Stéphane Mallarmé*, p. 27.

³*Antología lírica de Julio Herrera y Reissig*, p. 139.

⁴For a similar opinion see Y. Pino Saavedra, *La poesía de Julio Herrera y Reissig* . . . , p. 55.

⁵Svend Johansen, *Le Symbolisme*, pp. 75, 289.

⁶Paul Claudel, "La Catastrophe d'Igitur," *La Nouvelle Revue Française*, XXVII (1926), 534.

⁷Paul Valéry, "Littérature," *La Nouvelle Revue Française*, XXVI (1926), 674.

⁸For a discussion of this point see A. G. Lehmann, *The Symbolist Aesthetic in France* (1885-1895), pp. 162-165.

⁹*Ibid.*, p. 211, note.

¹⁰See Carlos Roxlo, *Historia crítica de la literatura uruguaya*, VII, 34.

¹¹Warren Ramsey, "Pound, Laforgue, and Dramatic Structure," *Comparative Literature*, III (1951), 56.

NOTES TO CHAPTER IV

¹Pedro Salinas, *Literatura española siglo XX*, p. 23.

²Herrera y Reissig, *Prosas*, p. 141.

³Lauxar, "El soneto 'Alba triste,'" in Julio Herrera y Reissig, *Antología lírica* . . . , p. 98.

⁴Jacopo Sannazaro, *Arcadia*, p. 70.

NOTES TO CHAPTER V

[1] Jorge Luis Borges, *Inquisiciones*, p. 144.
[2] The "fruta de ajena cerca" derives from Garcilaso's famous lines:

> Flérida, para mí dulce y sabrosa
> más que la fruta del cercado ajeno.

[3] "El banco del suplicio," "La estrella del destino," "El camino de las lágrimas," "La gota amarga," "La sombra dolorosa," "Luna de miel," "La reconciliación," "Decoración heráldica," "La violeta," and "La novicia," later included in *Los parques abandonados*, Part I, and "La ausencia meditativa," in Part II.
[4] Amado Alonso, *Ensayo sobre la novela histórica...*, pp. 298-303.

NOTES TO CHAPTER VI

[1] José Pedro Díaz, "Contactos entre Julio Herrera y Reissig y la poesía francesa," *Anales de la Universidad* (Montevideo), no. 162 (1948), p. 64.
[2] Y. Pino Saavedra, *La poesía de Julio Herrera y Reissig*, p. 60.
[3] Herrera y Reissig, *Prosas*, p. 117.

BIBLIOGRAPHY

WORKS OF JULIO HERRERA Y REISSIG

Antología lírica de Julio Herrera y Reissig, ed. by C. Sábat Ercasty and Manuel de Castro. Santiago de Chile, 1939.
"De *Los maitines de la noche* (que aparecerá en París)," *Vida Moderna* (Montevideo), XI (1903), 44-51.
"Epílogo Wagneriano a 'La Política de Fusión,'" *Vida Moderna*, X (1902), 19-63.
Epílogo Wagneriano a "La Política de Fusión." Montevideo, 1943.
Los éxtasis de la montaña. La Plata, 1943.
Los éxtasis de la montaña y otros poemas escogidos. Introduction by Francisco González Guerrero. Mexico, 1917.
"Introducción," in Carlos López Rocha, *Palideces y púrpuras, versos.* Buenos Aires, 1905.
La Nueva Atlántida (Montevideo), periodical edited by Julio Herrera y Reissig, May and June, 1907.
Obras completas. Montevideo: O. M. Bertani, 1910-1913. 5 vols.
Opalos. Buenos Aires, 1919.
Páginas escogidas de Julio Herrera y Reissig. Introduction by Juan Mas y Pi. Barcelona, 1919.
Los parques abandonados. Montevideo, 1919.
Los peregrinos de piedra. Preface by Rufino Blanco Fombona. Paris, 1914 (?).
Poesías. Madrid, 1911. It contains "Julio Herrera y Reissig; conferencia pronunciada por F. Villaespesa," pp. 9-36.
Poesías completas. Introduction by Guillermo de Torre, Buenos Aires, 1942.
Prosas: crítica, cuentos, comentarios. Introduction by Vincente A. Salaverri. Montevideo, 1918.

La *Revista* (Montevideo), periodical edited by Julio Herrera y Reissig, November 5, 1899, to July 10, 1900.

"La sombra," *Pegaso* (Montevideo), May, 1919, pp. 412-419; October, 1920, pp. 146-150.

STUDIES ON HERRERA Y REISSIG AND

OTHER WORKS CONSULTED

Alonso, Amado. *Ensayo sobre la novela histórica. El modernismo en La gloria de don Ramiro.* Buenos Aires, 1942.

Antuña, José Gervasio. "La calle del poeta," *Litterae.* Paris, 1926.

—. "Rubén Darío y Julio Herrera y Reissig," *ibid.*

Baudelaire, Charles. *Œuvres complètes.* Paris, 1925-1926. 7 vols.

Blanco Fombona, Rufino. "Julio Herrera y Reissig," *El modernismo y los poetas modernistas.* Madrid, 1929.

—. "El poeta uruguayo Julio Herrera y Reissig," *Sol* (Madrid), June 6, 1923.

Bordoli, D. L. "Julio Herrera y Reissig," *Revista Nacional* (Montevideo), VII (1945), 217-221.

Borges, Jorge Luis. *Inquisiciones.* Buenos Aires, 1925.

—. "Palabras finales," in Idelfonso Pereda Valdés, *Antología de la moderna poesía uruguaya.* Buenos Aires, 1927.

—. *El tamaño de mi esperanza.* Buenos Aires, 1926.

Brenes Mesén, Roberto. *Crítica americana.* Costa Rica, 1936.

Brughetti, Romualdo. "Julio Herrera y Reissig," *18 poetas del Uruguay.* Montevideo, 1937.

Bula Píriz, Roberto. *Herrera y Reissig (1875-1910). Vida y obra. Bibliografía. Antología.* New York, 1952.

Candia Marc, Delfor. "La poesía de Herrera y Reissig," *Nosotros* (Buenos Aires), XVIII (1942), 82-88.

Cansinos-Asséns, Rafael. "Herrera y Reissig," *Poetas y prosistas del novecientos.* Madrid, 1919.

—. "Julio Herrera y Reissig," *La nueva literatura.* Madrid, 1927. Vol. III.

—. "El modernismo. Los poetas: Herrera Reissig," *Verde y dorado en las letras americanas.* Madrid, 1947.

Casal, Julián del. *Poesías completas.* La Habana, 1945.
Casal, Julio J. *Exposición de la poesía uruguaya.* Montevideo, 1940.
Claudel, Paul. "La Catastrophe d'Igitur," *La Nouvelle Revue Française,* XXVII (1926), 531-536.
Coester, Alfred Lester. *Anthology of the Modernista Movement.* Boston and New York, 1924.
—. *The Literary History of Spanish America.* New York, 1916.
Colquhoun, Elizabeth. "New Interpretations of Spanish Poetry," *Bulletin of Spanish Studies,* XXI (1944), 39.
—. "Notes on French Influences in the Work of Julio Herrera y Reissig," *ibid.,* pp. 145-158.
Craig, George Dundas. *The Modernist Trend in Spanish American Poetry.* Berkeley, 1934.
La Cruz del Sur (Montevideo), no. 29, dedicated to Herrera y Reissig.
Daireaux, Max. *Panorama de la littérature hispano-américaine.* Paris, 1930.
Darío, Rubén. *Escritos inéditos de Rubén Darío.* Recogidos de periódicos de Buenos Aires y anotados por E. K. Mapes. New York, 1938.
—. *Obras completas.* Madrid, 1919. 21 vols.
De Vitis, Michael Angelo. *Florilegio del Parnaso americano.* Barcelona, 1927?
Díaz, José Pedro. "Contactos entre Julio Herrera y Reissig y la poesía francesa," *Anales de la Universidad* (Montevideo), no. 162, pp. 51-68.
Díez Canedo, Enrique. *Letras de América.* Mexico, 1944.
Donoso González, Francisco. *Al margen de la poesía, ensayos.* Paris, 1927.
Duplessis, Gustavo. "Julián del Casal," *Revista Bimestre Cubana* (La Habana), LIV (1944), 31-75, 140-170, 241-283.
Eliot, T. S. *The Sacred Wood.* London, 1928.
Englekirk, John Eugene. *Edgar Allan Poe in Hispanic Literatures.* New York, 1934.
Figueira, Gastón. "Julio Herrera y Reissig," *Sombra de la estatua.* Buenos Aires, 1923.
Filartigas, Juan M. "Julio Herrera y Reissig," *Artistas del Uruguay.* Montevideo, 1923.
—. "Julio Herrera y Reissig," *Mapa de la poesía.* Montevideo, 1930.
Flores, Mora Magela. *Julio Herrera y Reissig (Estudio biográfico).* Montevideo, 1947.
Fusco Sansone, Nicolás. *Antología y crítica de la literatura uruguaya.* Montevideo, 1940.

García Calderón, Ventura, and Hugo D. Barbagelata. "Julio Herrera y Reissig," *Semblanzas de América*. Madrid, 1920.
—. "La literatura uruguaya (1757-1917)," *Revue Hispanique* (Paris), XL (1917), 415-542.
Goldberg, Isaac. *Studies in Spanish American Literature*. New York, 1920.
González, Juan Antonio. *Dos figuras cumbres del Uruguay. Florencio Sánchez: En el teatro. Julio Herrera y Reissig: En la poesía*. Colonia, 1944.
Grecia, Pablo de. "Un homenaje a Julio Herrera y Reissig," *Prosas*. Montevideo, 1918.
Guillén, Jorge. *La poética de Bécquer*. New York, 1943.
Gutiérrez Nájera, Manuel. "El cruzamiento en literatura," *Revista Azul* (Mexico), September 9, 1894, pp. 289-292.
Henríquez Ureña, Max. *Rodó y Rubén Darío*. La Habana, 1918.
Henríquez Ureña, Pedro. *Literary Currents in Hispanic America*. Cambridge, Mass. 1945.
—. *La versificación irregular en la poesía castellana*, 2d ed. Madrid, 1933.
Herrera y Reissig, Herminia. "A Uruguayan Boy," *Bulletin of the Pan American Union*, LXXVIII (1944), 102-103.
—. *Vida íntima de Julio Herrera y Reissig*. Montevideo, 1943.
Herrera y Reissig, Teodoro. "Algunos aspectos ignorados de la vida y la obra de Julio Herrera y Reissig," *Hiperión* (Montevideo). no. 87 (1943), pp. 2-14.
Holmes, Henry Alfred. *Spanish America in Song and Story*. New York, 1932.
Huret, Jules. *Enquête sur l'évolution littéraire*. Paris, 1894.
Ibáñez, Roberto. "Americanismo y modernismo," *Cuadernos americanos*, VII (1948), 230-252.
Jiménez, Juan Ramón. "Crisis del espíritu en la poesía española contemporánea," *Nosotros* (Buenos Aires), XII (1940), 165-182.
Johansen, Svend. *Le Symbolisme*. Copenhagen, 1945.
Lauxar (O. Crispo Acosta). "Julio Herrera y Reissig," *Motivos de crítica hispanoamericanos*. Montevideo, 1914.
Lee, Muna. "Contemporary Spanish American Poetry," *North American Review*, CCXIX (1924), 687.
Lehmann, A. G. *The Symbolist Aesthetic in France (1885-1895)*. London, 1950.
Levillier, Roberto. "Herrera y Reissig y Leopoldo Lugones," *Hommage à Ernest Martinenche*. Paris, 1939?
López Morillas, Juan. "El *Azul* de Rubén Darío. ¿Galicismo mental o lingüístico?" *Revista Hispánica Moderna*, X (1944), 9-14.

Luisi, Luisa. "The Literature of Uruguay in the Year of the Constitutional Centenary," *Bulletin of the Pan American Union,* LXIV (1930), 655-695.
Mallarmé, Stéphane. *Œuvres complètes.* Paris, 1945.
Mapes, Edwin K. "Recent Research on the *Modernista* Poets," *Hispanic Review,* IV (1936), 47-54.
Martínez Cuitiño, Vicente. "Julio Herrera y Reissig (En el primer aniversario de su muerte)," *Nosotros,* V (1911), 208-210.
Mas y Pi, Juan. "Julio Herrera y Reissig," *Nosotros,* XIII (1914), 234-265.
Montero Bustamante, Raúl. *El Parnaso oriental.* Montevideo, 1905.
Nosotros, VII (May-June, 1938), number dedicated to Leopoldo Lugones. Pertinent articles by Leónidas Vidal Peña, Víctor Pérez Petit, Emilio Frugoni, and José Pereira Rodríguez.
Núñez Olano, Andrés. "El sol de los muertos," *Nuestra América* (Buenos Aires), no. 35 (October, 1922), pp. 394-400.
Núñez Regueiro, M. "Contemporary Uruguayan Literature," *Inter America,* III (1920), 305-315.
Onís y Sánchez, Federico de. *Antología de la poesía española e hispanoamericana (1882-1932).* Madrid, 1934.
Oribe, Emilio. "Nota sobre Herrera y Reissig—Lugones," *Hiperión* (Montevideo), no. 73 (1942), pp. 17-20.
—. *Poética y plástica.* Montevideo, 1930.
Pereda Valdés, Idelfonso. *Antología de la moderna poesía uruguaya (1900-1927).* Buenos Aires, 1927.
Pereira Rodríguez, José. "De 'La Revista' a 'La Nueva Atlántida,'" *Número* (Montevideo), II (1950), 293-299.
Pérez Galdós, Benito. *Zumalacárregui.* Madrid, 1898.
Phillips, Allen W. "La metáfora en la obra de Julio Herrera y Reissig," *Revista Iberoamericana,* XVI (1950), 31-48.
Pillement, G., and de la Nible, J. "Les extases de la montagne: Le Réveil, La Flûte, Le Retour des champs," *Revue de l'Amérique Latine,* VII (1924).
—. "Quatre Sonnets: Le Réveil, L'Eglise, Le Potager, La Masse Candide," *ibid.,* pp. 37-38.
Pinilla, Norberto. "Lírica de Julio Herrera y Reissig," *Cinco poetas.* Santiago de Chile, 1937.
Pino Saavedra, Y. *La poesía de Julio Herrera y Reissig. Sus temas y su estilo.* Santiago de Chile, 1932.
Ramírez, Octavio. "El humorismo de Julio Herrera y Reissig," *La Nación,* August 22, 1925.
Ramsey, Warren. "Pound, Laforgue, and Dramatic Structure," *Comparative Literature,* III (1951), 47-56.

Reyes, Alfonso. "Mallarmé en espagnol," *Revue de Littérature Comparée,* XII (1932), 546-568.
Reyles, Carlos. "Julio Herrera y Reissig," *Historia sintética de la literatura uruguaya.* Montevideo, 1931. Vol. I, Chap. viii (Contribution of Carlos Sábat Ercasty).
Rodríguez Marín, Francisco, ed. *Obras de Pedro de Espinosa.* Madrid, 1909.
Rodríguez Monegal, Emir. *José E. Rodó en el novecientos.* Montevideo, 1950.
Ronchi March, Carlos A. "Julio Herrera y Reissig," *Nosotros,* XVIII (1942), 285-293.
Roxlo, Carlos. *Historia crítica de la literatura uruguaya.* Montevideo, 1916. Vol. VII.
—. "Julio Herrera y Reissig," *Revista Nacional* (Montevideo), VIII (1945), 286-300.
Salinas, Pedro. *Literatura española siglo XX.* Mexico, 1941
Samain, Albert. *Œuvres complètes.* Paris, 1924. 3 vols.
Sánchez, Luis Alberto. *Nueva historia de la literatura americana.* Buenos Aires, 1943.
Sanín Cano, Baldomero. "José Asunción Silva," *Revista de las Indias* (Bogotá), XXVIII (1946), 161-178.
Sannazaro, Jacopo. *Arcadia.* Turin, 1926.
Silva, José Asunción. *Prosas y versos,* ed. Carlos García Prada. Mexico, 1942.
Silva Uzcátegui, R. D. *Historia crítica del modernismo.* Barcelona, 1925.
Solari Amondarain, I. "Hace veinticinco años se acalló la voz del cantor de la Torre de los Panoramas, " *La Prensa,* December 22, 1935.
Spitzer, Leo. *La enumeración caótica en la poesía moderna.* Buenos Aires, 1945.
Suárez Calimano, E. "Orientaciones de la literatura hispanoamericana en los últimos veinte años," *Nosotros,* LVII (1927), 285-314.
Thibaudet, Albert. *La Poésie de Stéphane Mallarmé.* Paris, 1926.
Torre, Guillermo de. "El pleito Lugones—Herrera y Reissig," *Argentina Libre,* March 12, 1942.
—. "Valor y medida de Julio Herrera y Reissig," *La Nación,* February 8, 1942.
—. "Valor y medida de Julio Herrera y Reissig," *La aventura y el orden.* Buenos Aires, 1943.
Torres-Ríoseco, Arturo. *The Epic of Latin American Literature.* New York, 1942.
—. "Las teorías poéticas de Poe y el caso de José Asunción Silva," *Hispanic Review,* XVIII (1950), 319-327.
Umphrey, G. W. "Fifty Years of Modernism in Spanish

American Poetry," *Modern Language Quarterly*, I (1940), 101-114.
Unamuno y Jugo, Miguel de. *Paz en la guerra*. Madrid, 1897.
Valéry, Paul. "Littérature," *La Nouvelle Revue Française*, XXVI (1926), 671-675.
—. "Situation de Baudelaire," *Variété II*. Paris, 1930.
Vela, Arqueles. *Teoría literaria del modernismo*. Mexico, 1949.
Vilariño, Idea. "Julio Herrera y Reissig," *Número*, II (1950) 118-161.
—. *Julio Herrera y Reissig, seis años de poesía*. Montevideo, 1950.
Walsh, Thomas, ed. *Hispanic Anthology*. New York, 1920.
—. "Julio Herrera y Reissig, a Disciple of E. A. Poe," *Poet Lore*, XXXIII (1922), 601-607.
Zum Felde, Alberto. "Contemporary Uruguayan Poetry," *Inter America*, IX (1925), 62-84.
—. *Indice de la poesía uruguaya contemporánea*. Santiago, 1935.
—. "Julio Herrera y Reissig," *Proceso intelectual del Uruguay y crítica de su literatura*. Montevideo, 1930. II, 115-150.
—. *La literatura del Uruguay*. Buenos Aires, 1939.

INDEX

Baudelaire, C., 4, 5, 6, 10, 20, 25-29, 39, 43-45, 56, 85, 86
Bécquer, G. A., 3, 4, 6, 15, 80
Bouilhet, L., 6

Campoamor, R. de, 3, 6
Carreras, R. de las, 17, 21
Casal, J. del, 4-5
Coppée, F., 4, 5, 6, 10
Costumbrismo, 3

Darío, R., 2, 5, 7, 8-14, 16, 18, 20, 21-25, 27, 28, 31, 33, 34, 55, 78, 86, 87, 90, 92
Decadence, 2, 4, 6, 7, 8, 10, 11, 12, 14-20, 25, 27, 30, 32, 56, 84, 85
Díaz, L., 7
Díaz Mirón, S., 7, 9

Gautier, J., 5, 9
Gautier, T., 4, 5, 9
Gil, R., 7
Goncourt, E. and J., 10
González Prada, M., 7
Gutiérrez Nájera, M., 4, 5-6

Heine, H., 6, 21, 77—78
Heredia, J. M., 4, 5, 10
Hugo, V., 2, 3, 6, 9, 22
Huysmans, J. K., 5, 19, 43

Leconte de Lisle, 4, 9
Loti, P., 4, 5, 9
Lugones, L., 16, 33

Mallarmé, S., 6, 9, 11, 12, 16, 19, 20, 25, 28-33, 37, 40, 47, 48, 50, 52, 53, 54

Martí, J., 3-4, 8
Mendès, C., 5, 6, 9, 10
Moréas, J., 11, 19
Musset, A. de, 5, 6, 86

Nordau, M., 7

Othón, M. J., 7

Parnasse, 2, 4, 8, 9, 11, 14, 16, 89
Poe, E. A., 6, 20, 25-29 *passim*, 39, 40

Quiroga, H., 17

Realism, 3, 15
Reina, M., 7
Rimbaud, A., 6, 20, 49
Rodó, J. E., 15, 16, 18
Romanticism, 2, 3, 4, 10, 14, 15, 20, 21, 22, 52, 55, 56
Rossetti, D. G., 6, 11, 12
Rueda, S., 7

Samain, A., 21, 30, 32-39, 58, 61
Sánchez, F., 17
Silva, J. A., 4, 6-7, 8
Symbolism, 2, 3, 8, 9, 11, 12, 16, 18, 19-20, 25, 30, 32, 39-54 *passim*, 55, 91

Valéry, P., 19, 20, 50, 53
Verlaine, P., 5, 6, 7, 11, 12, 16, 19, 20, 25, 30-31, 33, 77
Villiers de l'Isle-Adam, 6, 19

Whitman, W., 3, 9

Zorrilla de San Martín, J., 15

www.ingramcontent.com/pod-product-compliance
Lightning Source LLC
Chambersburg PA
CBHW021715230426
43668CB00008B/839